Redwood Writers
2022 Poetry Anthology

Crossroads

Les Bernstein and Fran Claggett-Holland
Co-editors

Betty Les and Jory Bellsey
Editorial Assistants

Linda L. Reid
Board Liaison

An anthology of poetry
by Redwood Writers
A branch of the
California Writers Club

Redwood Writers 2022 Poetry Anthology:
Crossroads

Editors
Les Bernstein and Fran Claggett-Holland

© 2022 by Redwood Writers
All rights reserved

ISBN: 979-8-9853503-1-9

Library of Congress Control Number: 2022908206

Book design
by Jo-Anne Rosen
Wordrunner Publishing Services

Cover art
by Christine MacDonald

Published by Redwood Writers Press
PO Box 4687
Santa Rosa, California 95402

Contents

Introduction *1*
Acknowledgements *3*

Featured Writers

Barbara Armstrong
- J *7*

Jean Wong
- My Name *9*

Dana Rodney
- Collect My Dust *11*

Patricia Nelson
- Cassandra *12*

Dana Rodney
- Wildfire Elegy *14*

Jo Ann Smith
- Purple Dust *16*

Crossroads

Barbara Armstrong
- To Capture a Road Runner *21*
- Our Halcyon Days *23*
- Never in this Lifetime will I *25*
- After the Punctuation Purge *27*

Judy Baker
- Threads *28*
- Poetry Stutters *29*

Kitty Baker
- The Majesty of Things Unseen *30*

Margaret Barkley
- Anatomy of Fear *31*
- Lion the Size of Texas *33*
- Brothel of Wonder *34*
- You Don't Know What You Have *36*
- Wet Trout *37*

JoAnn Bell
- Love is a Hat *38*
- Childhood Remembered *39*

Jory Bellsey
- The Way Back *40*
- The Wait *41*
- Noises *43*
- Gone *44*
- Seeds *45*

Les Bernstein
- Les attempts a pantoum *46*
- Today's News *47*
- Autumnal Equinox *48*
- Caesura *49*
- Passage *50*

Skye Blaine
- stardust *51*
- threshold *53*

Laura Blatt
- Wandering Through the Apocalypse *54*

Abby Bogomolny
- because I turn on the light switch she thinks I make the sun come out *55*
- Life of the Yenta *56*
- Looting *57*

Angel Booth
- Feb 2019 .... *58*
- Discreet *59*

Catharine Bramkamp
- The Emperor *60*
- The Empress *61*
- The Fool *62*
- The High Priestess *63*
- Death *64*

Robbi Sommers Bryant
- Loving a Sociopath *65*

Marilyn Campbell
- Resolutions *66*

Simona Carini
- Walking Along 156th Avenue NE in a City
  That Is Not at War *67*
- Responsibility *68*
- Train Rides from Perugia, Italy *70*

Fran Claggett-Holland
- In Times Like These. *72*
- Tabula Rasa *75*
- adagio cantabile *76*
- At Death *78*
- Until *80*

Penelope Anne Cole
- Beloved Beauty Mine *81*

Marlene Cullen
- Winter I *82*
- Winter II *83*

Joseph Cutler
- When Are We Really Together? *84*
- An Apple a Day *85*
- Crystals *86*
- Unfinished Business *87*

Patrice Deems
- Taureans *89*

Paul DeMarco
- Larkspur Ferry on the Fourth of July 2021 . . . . *90*
- The North Star *92*
- Transfiguration, Sonoma October *94*
- Appropriate Technology *95*

Nancy Dougherty
- To Escape the Everyday *97*
- Layers of Love *99*

Anita Erola
- Mourning Doves *101*
- The Lemon Cake Dance *102*
- No. 2085 .... *104*

Rebecca Evert
- Lament *105*

Robin Gabbert
- Dental Hygiene *106*
- Nose Job *108*
- BPS (Blank Page Syndrome) *110*
- Posthumous Epithalamion for Ethel & Sid *111*

Christina Gleason
- Evering *113*

Joan Goodreau
- When Will It End? *114*
- Before and After Spring *115*
- Fire Season in Bidwell Park *116*
- Exposed *117*
- Vet. *118*

Chlele Gummer
- Sept 2020 .... *119*

Karen Hayes
- Stones *120*

Pamela Heck
- Warrior with a Walker *122*
- Coming Storm *124*
- Genesis *125*

J. L. Henker
- Island *126*

Basha Hirschfeld
- David loves rocks *127*
- Running through the Rain *129*
- To My Writing Class *130*
- boomerang trajectory *131*

Jon Jackson
- Stars On A Rainy Night *133*

Mara Johnstone
- The Mundane Years *134*
- A Variety of Earthlings *135*

Karl Kadie
- Night Muse. *136*
- Grace. *137*

Anne Keck
- Victoriana Apologizes *139*

Briahn Kelly-Brennan
- All Along The Serious Day *140*
- Slow Drift of an Untethered Mind on a Sunny Afternoon *141*

Crissi Langwell
- Wolf Howl. *142*

Shawn Langwell
- Spring *143*

Betty Les
- Trees and Other Friends *144*
- Last Stand *146*
- The Stirring *147*
- Holy Water *148*
- Rain Sharpens Memory *149*

Sherrie Lovler
- Persimmons *151*
- Ode to Nightshade, My Cat *152*
- Grove Street Is Less of a Grove Today *154*
- Brothers. *156*
- Everything New *157*

Roger Lubeck
- Tenderloin. *158*

Steven Lubliner
- Mudder *160*
- Fodder *161*

Marianne Lyon
- Starlings *162*
- You think I am lost *164*
- I look at you *165*

Elaine Maikovska
- Time *167*

Catherine Montague
- In the Aquarium *168*

Rod Morgan
- Coastline *170*

Jennie Orvino
- Nature Walk with Simone Whitecloud *171*
- For the memorial *172*
- If I found a sweetheart *173*
- A Cockatiel Named for Wolfgang Amadeus Mozart . *174*

Amy Pane
- Birthday 2014 .... *175*
- Reflections *177*
- Exhaustion *178*
- Dance for 2020 .... *179*

Linda Loveland Reid
- Vortex of Me *181*

Jane Rinaldi
- Winter Blues *183*

Margaret Rooney
- Intonations *184*
- Parrhesia *185*
- Nights These Days *187*
- Somedays the World is Too Rich to be Eaten ... *189*
- That Far Thing So Near *191*

Janice Rowley
- Themes *192*

Dimitri Rusov-Morningstar
- Meditation *193*

Kathleen Scavone
- Blossom Fall *194*
- Clouds. *195*

Florentia Scott
- Saint-Michel d'Aiguilhe *196*

Scott Sherman
- Crowned by the Corona *197*
- Ode to That Spark *198*

Jo Ann Smith
- Grave Matters *199*
- Emergency. *201*
- The Only Girl *204*
- I Never Saw It Coming *206*
- Coming To My Senses. *207*

Linda Stamps
- Dominant Chord *209*
- Artifacts *211*
- Departure *212*
- Glyphs. *214*
- Twelve for Dinner *215*

Steve Trenam
- At the Far End of a Sturdy Branch *216*
- Silence *218*
- Lavender *219*
- Stream of Consciousness *221*
- Parabola *222*

Judith Vaughn
- Shiva Birds *224*
- Day in the Country *225*
- A Murder of Crows *226*
- I Have No Prayers *227*
- Murmurations *228*

Marilyn Wolters
- Amanda. *229*

Jaime Zukowski
- In Memory Care *230*
- Love's Lack *231*
- Call *233*
- The Male of the Species *234*
- Elegy for Question Mark Oak *235*

Fran Claggett-Holland and Les Bernstein
- A Journey Lighted by the Aurora Polaris *236*

Appendices

Poet Biographies. *239*
Artist's Statement: Christine MacDonald *251*
Redwood Branch History. *252*
Redwood Writers Presidents. *253*
Awards *254*

Introduction

> "We have to get used to the idea that at the most important crossroads in our life there are no signs."
> — Ernest Hemingway

One of the literal definitions for crossroads is "the point where two roads meet." However, it could be used metaphorically to mean an important moment of choice. In 2015 I was invited to judge a Redwood Writers Poetry Contest. That was the day my road crossed with Fran Claggettt-Holland and the Redwood Writers. I did not know at that time how important that choice to be a judge would be. I also did not know the many wonderful poets I would come to encounter and come to love (especially Fran). I thank all the poets who appear in *Crossroads* for taking a moment of choice to write their poems, fill out the submission form and push send. Here are the poets and their poems in the 2022 *Crossroads* anthology. Speaking for Fran and myself, we are deeply moved that all our paths have crossed.

— Les Bernstein

Acknowledgements

The Redwood Writers who have made this book possible are, of course, the writers who have sent their poems to us. Without them, there would not be this book. In addition, we want to acknowledge the following members:

Our impeccable editorial assistants: Betty Les and Jory Bellsey
Our book designer and patient saint: Jo-Anne Rosen
Our meticulous webmaster: Joelle Burnette
Our cover artist and friend: Christine MacDonald
Our lovely jack of all trades: Linda Loveland Reid

Our gratitude to them and to the Redwood Writers Board of Directors for again supporting this project.

Featured Writers

Our Featured Writers and Winners of the 2021 Redwood Writers Poetry Contest

First Place
Barbara Armstrong

J

You never waved good-bye.
Sitting upright in the passenger seat of
your daughter's white sedan,
you held your pillow close to your chest,
looked neither toward our house nor away
but fixed your focus straight ahead
into your own uncertain destiny.
The gate clanged shut. I wonder. . .
did you see me wave good-bye.

On the deck downstairs
your tarnished watering can sits
dry as last week's yesterdays.
Heavy in their oaken barrels
your precious Chinese Jades extend
their sturdy arms in all directions.
Totems of abundance and good fortune
still flank the door of your hide-away
now left strangely open.

Beyond the rail, I see what you
must have always noticed
as the Summers waned—
that gnarled apple tree enacting
the final episode of its season.
So full of promise in July,

the Gravensteins now spill
their knobs of gold and bronze
across the stubbled hill.

The scent of fermentation draws the doe
who lifts her head with calm,
reflective eyes to take me in.
The feral fox that used to sidle
past your bedroom door has
taken to sleeping in your outdoor chair;
its tell-tale paw prints
claim the cushions now
you are gone.

The whir of flight shivers the redwood branches. . .
A feather drifts through loosened air.
Down from the breast of a mourning dove
descends in languid motion, waving
side to side like the gloved hand of a queen.
It rides a shallow tide
and comes to rest upon my palm
like an afterthought
or a talisman.

Second Place

Jean Wong

My Name

in first grade
my teacher wrote
on the blackboard because
I was arranging my crayons
and hadn't heard her say:

Put your hands in your lap and look at me

the name   sprawled   like   white
       ghost   lines   was
                      left to
                screech

all morning
the next day more shame
was smeared

I see Joan is paying attention today

Could I have stood, told her and
                         myself
before splayed on the board

                I was there
                my crayon colors
     blinking   like   flower   stalks

afterwards

                                        I disappeared

                                                      into a thick choke

                                                                  of chalk

                  it took years to re-surface
                  wary   cautious

                        attentive

Third Place
Dana Rodney

Collect My Dust

God
when I die
collect my dust
but do not remake me
a woman
make of me a stone
a rock reposing
on the lap of the earth
unnoticed
elemental
resplendent in the cold moonlight
empty of utterance
of no particular use
except perhaps to toss
into the sea
one ecstatic splash
the only word
I speak.

Honorable Mentions

Patricia Nelson

Cassandra

i.

An image rises, walled and still.
My city's towers glow:
wicks already burning.

My sight slides over it
like small clear shapes of rain
showing deaths of many sizes.

My own death—
bright to me.

ii.

Mist rotates like the cold stars,
like the white and circling sea:
A site where outcomes writhe.

I can see the war, the spoiled city,
the wet dirt where the fallen
will glitter like violets.

But no one listens when I speak.
Not soldiers, not the crying, folded girls
about to twist on shoulders.

iii.

Is my voice too high, too crowded?
Is it churning like a sky that tries
to utter all it knows at once:

Its wilderness of distance
the stuttered grief of birdsong,
the loneliness of knowledge.

Why must I go among the deaf—
those lovely, heedless, unwarned things
on their way to glow and die?

iv.

Is it always so, oh god of light,
that those about to fall
are cursed with disbelief?

God of sky, I cannot hold your gift:
your wheeling eye, the weight of it,
without its wing of distance.

Dana Rodney

Wildfire Elegy

I used to think I could rely on the days
one following the other so faithfully
the innocent breath of morning
the folding petals of night
the years flowing by like rushing water

Nature's mood is generally predictable
except for the periodic cataclysm:
a meteor annihilating the dinosaurs
tectonic plates colliding
and depositing a mountain range
but you never think of a cataclysm interrupting
your own placid days
you never think
you
are the dinosaur

You never think about how
you are just carbon rearranged
something combustible
how everything you've collected in a lifetime
is just more fuel to a flame
that delicate painting of poppies

I hung on the wall wherever I lived
consumed as greedily
as a forgotten sock under my bed,
my mother's thumb-stained recipes,
a lover's penciled poem,
that nut-brown guitar that played a thousand songs,
the carefully-tended jasmine,

my old cowboy boots still stained,
with the sweat of my youth,
even
my mother's ashes that rested on a shelf
now twice burned
mingle in the rubble.

Now I no longer belong to a place
the objects that housed my memories have combusted
I alone am left to remember the things
when I thought the things would be left
to remember me.

Jo Ann Smith

Purple Dust

Sometimes I pray
not knowing if prayers
are anything more
than a sigh
carried by the wind
into nothing

before my life is over
will some omniscient narrator
whose eyes see light and dark
in their original colors
reveal the mysteries of life
before, now and after

I have felt an untold presence,
but don't believe it's real
I have gathered at the river,
but never witnessed angels dancing
worshiped at the mountain
never reaching higher ground

so done am I
twisting in ambivalence
my own tapestry
of rainbow-colored silk
drifting unspooled
in a blur of purple dust

so tired am I
traveling back and forth
on tumbledown terrain

across a bridge of my own mistakes
looking for the River Jordan
with its promise of deliverance

can it be enough
to cultivate a heart that beats
in rhythm with a universal pulse
and keep a steady grip
on the edge of this ancient rock
until with wonder I let it go

Crossroads

Barbara Armstrong

To Capture a Road Runner

for Amy Sarratt

you *could* get up at daybreak
pack the pockets of your khaki vest
with pencils   sketchpad   a field guide from Audubon
with facts and colored plates
strap on a backpack and drape from your neck
a four-star camera with a telephoto lens

or you *could* stay home wrapped in
yesterday's pajamas open the sliding door
and settle at your piano keyboard
as spaces open up in both your hemispheres
initiate a melody from deep within
unrehearsed and free of expectation
perhaps a hybrid blend of Bach etudes with
fickle interludes of Amadeus and nouveau Sarratt
play it soft and easy the way you like to do
so as not to undermine the desert quietude
In time you'll feel a subtle shift
sense a wild presence lingering

tail feathers on alert
top-knot slightly at a tilt
an attitude of listening
your image is held captive
in a jeweled glistening eye

that elusive bird you sought
is standing at your threshold looking in
not a piece of common yard art
or some lightweight feather duster

but a curious warm-blooded
creature like yourself
a sentient spirit with
an earnest ear for music

Barbara Armstrong

Our Halcyon Days

for Tre Ford 1927-2021

out on the job-site we'd often find
you lugging two-by-fours to the radial saw
calculating to the blade's width
the precision of each cut
timbers and sheets of plywood
compliant to your command

you led an unlikely crew of women
in striped overalls apron
pockets equipped with tapes
flat carpenter pencils, number eights
bullet levels, sixteen ounce
hammers slung from loops

you'd roust us out before daybreak
to obviate the torch of mid-day sun
we were the ones who held the other end
who helped to raise the walls and thread the wires
we'd scramble ladders to the roof
cut loose and spread the bundled shingles

you taught us how to sweat
the copper joints
connect the maze of water pipes
till rainbows gushed from
every tap and spigot

Anything worth doing
is worth doing well you'd say

as pink blankets showered fiberglass
on our hoods in the sweltering crawl space
as concrete hardened on the lips
of our rubber boots at sundown

These are our halcyon days
you would insist

and now my oldest-dearest friend
I'm sending all my faith and love
to tell you it's okay to move
from chairman of the board
to woman of the lift

from architect of dreams
to resident upstairs
from driving force
to one who must be driven

Those were our halcyon days
you always liked to reminisce

and yes
they were

Barbara Armstrong

Never in this Lifetime will I . . .

After Fran Claggett-Holland

build a tree house in the Amazon
among feather and twig
orchids woven in the walls
arboreal neighbor to a gang of howlers
companion to a three toed sloth

rent a fishing hut on Lake Ontario
bobbers   hooks   and buckets dangling-
one charmed opening to a world beneath the ice
one straight-backed chair
where I must practice patience and settle for solitaire

discern the origin of certain memories-
breathing smoky incense of the chambers of Lascaux
a scrap of common charcoal in my grip
as I trace the outline of my envisioned horse
on the cold canvas of permanence

spend unending days and nights
on the Steppes of Central Asia
in a felted woolen yurt marked
with the five symbols of the cosmos
fire, wind, water, metal, wood

warm my hands by an iron stove
redolent of boiled mutton,
five chap-cheeked children
nesting in my skirts
untamed horses grazing outside

surround myself with saltwater seas,
trek the Faroe Islands to where ice-fields
and lava flows convene, dream deep
beneath a dome of undulating green,
the satin sheets of arctic sky

Never in this lifetime
will I embark on a boat
built for one drifting down
a tributary to the sea
unencumbered
by need
of paddle
or compass
or company

Barbara Armstrong

After the Punctuation Purge

The poets retreat from the salon
expurgated poems in hand
kudos all 'round for a job well done,
but as you return for the empty plates
take note of the chaos you create

See there, an aggregate of periods like spent buckshot
come to a full stop along an apathetic wall.
Now what will serve to regulate your flow of words?

And there, parentheses, a torn hair net
rendered obsolete by absolute consensus.
*(But life is parenthetical; where would your stodgy stanzas be without
    our pertinent asides?)*

Plotting a hasty picket line around
the philodendron pot, excited exclamation points
goose-step their discontent.
No way! No way! No Way! No Way! they punctuate their foment.

Behind the silver curtain, commas flounder
like a pond of polliwogs after a rain of terror.
"Ungrateful bards," they mutter, *"and we were the ones who taught
    them how to breathe."*

poets in the kitchen consume
the last of the cashews
and head for home with neither
backward glance
nor hint of indentation

Judy Baker

Threads

words string warp
weft of memories packed tight
snugged against the beater bar inside my heart
mostly true stories twined
twisted threads interlock
painted rainbows woven
boundless palette unfurled
cascading colors bleed
emotion portraits fragile art
explored in quiet breath
meditation
infinity paused

Judy Baker

Poetry Stutters

Poetry stutters stops
arguing for release
bubbling fermenting oozing out of pores
insistent, incessant
words pop up
circle brain before bed
incandescent wordings play
whack a mole
surface, disappear, reappear
randomly repeat, gather, and disperse
lyrics mirror and reverse
in rhythms inferred

enigmatic observations
marking time in isolation
a swelling army united
marching columns split off
dazzling dance team choreography
as string pulls from inside my chest
rips away meaning, no way to digest
lingering lovely words
oscillate, jumble, pirouette
why do they hiccup inside my head?
tumbling acrobats unwilling participants
eluding attempts to record their patter
hiding, hidden hindering poetic perfection
suffocating
quarantined airtight
denied sunlight or completion
denied a sweet release

Kitty Baker

The Majesty of Things Unseen

It's forever raining in the bathroom
always coming down
between the slatted blinds
parsing air into waver slivers
that show its ever downward motion
infra, ultra, gamma, x rays acquiescing
to the draw of Earth's magma core
filling the center
nailing a crust of solid ground beneath our feet
ensuring against every misstep
a thousand invisible rays per nanosecond
we ought to feel the assault of it
piercing right on thru us
the body mass is nothing
no obstacle
just witness
as we sit
squinting out the window
in awe of its subtle majesty.

Margaret Barkley

Anatomy of Fear

when breath is short
like prey running,
and even at rest
hidden muscles grip
at nothing
lifting the body
out of sleep's peace

when the cloth wrapping frays
unravels
unable to hold anything
sinew and bone revealed

voices in disagreement —
everything will be fine
we will all die
just practice gratitude
infection is everywhere
good advice is everywhere
prepare for tragedy
envision perfect health
stay ahead of the pain
I will be fine
I am afraid

in the house of grief
real, but mostly imagined
not in the same room as death
not yet

is love the opposite
of this raw décor —
each day the invitation
to gather myself up
threadbare drape that I am
and hold myself dear
to find the small bloom of joy
at the center

Margaret Barkley

Lion the Size of Texas

If I am to live in this world
I must remember —
edges of things here
are not what they seem

and I am likely to awaken
in the quiet fog of morning
to find that a lion the size of Texas
has her paw on my chest
holding me firmly
with a weight thick with love
and light is pouring through me
like melted butter warm and golden,
a river rushing
through the curved banks
of my body

If I am to walk here
on solid ground,
shop for bananas
and talk on the phone to
earn my keep
I can only survive it
if I am also bathing
in the miracle
and the tragedy
of love

I am radiance in the shape of woman,
I am light held by soil and flesh —
tooth by tooth I will be eaten
by the unknowable mouth
till light is what remains

How do I speak of this?

Margaret Barkley

Brothel of Wonder

I am sitting at my desk
no clothes on
just my robe falling off one shoulder
open down the front
and slippers,
one of the best outfits
for writing poetry.

I am thinking of all the things
a responsible adult
would do right now, on this day—
a long list
but here I am.

How am I supposed to
carry on in the world
follow its rules
as if I am not a poet,
as if I could forget
that most of what we do
is not important at all
except as the miracle
that we are here to do it.

I want to live in a brothel of wonder,
where all I have to do
is love you and the whole world
and money arrives in the mail.
I want to talk with friends
and see light in their eyes.

I want to walk in trees on spongy earth
swim naked in rivers.
I want to live this life like a child, noticing.
I want to lounge around
barely clothed in soft things
and write it all down.
I want to give it back.

Margaret Barkley

You Don't Know What You Have

Curled in your arms
I am like soft dough rising
molded heavy against the bowl of your body.
The hum of you catches me by surprise
every time we touch.
If you knew the size of your heart
you would have no doubt about anything.

Like the heat of a quiet furnace,
like a sound too deep for human ears to hear,
or a slow shockwave still emanating from an ancient quake
you are packing power enough
to soothe and to surprise
even yourself.

You are the human version of comfort food —
warm chocolate,
chicken soup
bread slathered in butter —
nourishment that calms the nerves
and inspires great things.

If you knew your own strength
small birds would land on your shoulders and sing to you,
the cashier would swoon when you hand her the money.

Margaret Barkley

Wet Trout

My own sweet
heart
under the shadows
of a big rock
waiting
till the sun and the quiet
invite her out
Glistening,
rainbow-sided, sleek and firm
A good catch
Only the best bait
will do

JoAnn Bell

Love is a Hat

Love: That feeling you never thought you could live with
Until you had to live without it.
That memory you kept
Until it faded away.
That moment you conquer
Until it conquers you.
That emotion misunderstood
Until it is redefined.
That excitement which
Tastes new with every bite.
That vision eternally
Repeating itself.
That sound of an owl in the night
Asking to meet its shadow.
That experience described by
What it is not.
That touch which is anticipated.
That moment when
Nothing else matters.

JoAnn Bell

Childhood Remembered

Childhood:
When the future was
Another candle on the cake.
Father's love an umbrella to
Protect from the elements.
Mother a tightly spun ball of rules
To color the rebellion of youth.
Older brother Odysseus' hero of yearnings.
Pets who ran away and returned.
Everything new from blister to butterfly.
When books made us wake up to places
We had never been before.
No need to remember authors' names
As long as their stories were true.
When it felt perfectly natural to follow
A rabbit down his hole.
To change easily from one size to another.
I wanted to run away with Pinocchio
To miss my father who loved me too much.
Childhood:
A time to cut nature to fit society
Actions without anticipated outcome.
A time to learn the rules of the game.
An adventure that must end somewhere.

Jory Bellsey

The Way Back

how long can I ask you
to wait for me to arrive
my journey long and arduous
fraught with
disappointment
distraction and despair

taking many wrong turns
losing my direction
looking for a path to follow
confronting persistent stormy weather
impeding my way
stalling the progress I have made

suddenly the weather breaks
the skies brighten then clear
the road straightens and smooths
obstacles confronted and overcome
and challenges have been met
my angst begins to ease

I feel my journey is almost over
yet again I sense a change in the weather
the temperature drops suddenly
winds begin to blow and swirl
clouds collect and darken
indicating another storm is imminent

It's then that I wonder
will I ever find my way
back to myself
so
I can find my way
back to you

Jory Bellsey

The Wait

sometimes
it explodes like a volcano
spewing forth
giant plumes of smoke and ash
in uncontrollable ways

long pauses
until it oozes like lava flow
edging its way
immeasurably slow in progress
taking days weeks even months

rare instances
it rages like rapids
smashing against rocks
relentless and forceful
unstoppable and wild

at times
it trickles like a rill
meandering its way
eventually settling
in some languid pool

on occasion
it arrives with gale force winds
leaving havoc in its wake
and a large debris field
as far as the eye can see

often stagnating
like hot breezeless summer days
waiting for the slightest shift
signaling a welcome change
in the weather

all I can do
is wait
alert and ready
anxious for any sign
wondering

can it happen
will I be able to write
anything again
will the inspiration come
is there going to be a next time

Jory Bellsey

Noises

simplicity says
look in the mirror

avarice says
you need more

religion says
have faith follow me

ambition says
achieve more

doubt says
it will never happen

optimism says
any day now

confusion is
undecided

humility says
give it all away

intuition says
it's a conundrum

sadness says
its no use

I say
what are all these noises
I keep hearing

Jory Bellsey

Gone

no more where's my shoe
that he picks up
while crying at the back door
filling me with guilt every time I leave
the stare downs are gone now
his chin resting on the coffee table
eyes focused and intent
relentless
knowing I know what he wants
indignant when I bring a snack
without one for him
giving me the evil eye
that says
where's mine
always yielding
handing it over
saying last one
and waiting
as I watch him settle
for the night
we had an uncanny
connection to each other
touching
bound together
watching the TV
me knowing
we couldn't repeat this
over and over
for time indefinite

Jory Bellsey

Seeds

dreams of possibilities
have evaporated
like the last traces
of morning dew
surrendering
to the warmth of the day

meadows of wildflowers
swaying rhythmically
in a summer breeze
have wilted
leaving only remnants
of what once was

fragrances once abundant
in nature
must be synthesized
for our memories

photographs
now our only connection
to the wonders
and bounty
nature had intended

I am left wondering
how many seeds
will be left to sow

Les Bernstein

Les attempts a pantoum

remember the pastel of infinite sky
the sneaky sincerity of newly born clouds
forgiveness grows in this light
vanishes clots of petty concern

the sneaky sincerity of newly born clouds
laced with dreams and expectations
vanishes clots of petty concern
in the great swell of all that is

laced with dreams and expectations
forgiveness grows in this light
in the great swell of all that is
remember the pastel of infinite sky

Les Bernstein

Today's News

in a paradise of mediocrity
glaciers are melting
with the burn of indifference
sea levels rise

a disingenuous connecting of dots
a narrative of complacency
is sure to return our stardust
to an apathetic universe

despots may lay claim to lands
as if human ownership is possible
ultimately they will come and go
taking nothing with their passing

is it bitterly tragically funny
that all we have accomplished
is just another episode
of beget beget smite smite

Les Bernstein

Autumnal Equinox

dark so early
brackets the mood

a table set for one
suggests the absent

a gumbo of loss
made to be devoured

tedium mixed with spleen
seasoned with unease

Les Bernstein

Caesura

> *"What we cannot speak about we pass over in silence"*
>
> — Ludwig Wittgenstein

the season of your passing
is a newly charted world
awash in dingy colors
deafening the hollows

an unbreachable space
completes the aftermath
removes without absence
a fluent silence so loud

sorrow's very own enclosure
cannot communion beyond the sky
in the limits of language
it is said only wolves hear the stars

Les Bernstein

Passage

> *"No one can build you the bridge on which*
> *you, and only you, must cross the river of life"*
> — Friedrich Nietzsche

below a placid surface
of sunny yellow pursuit
there lies a human story
a narrative to provide order

between idea and substance
desire fragile as a soap bubble
gambles on consistency
glistens and floats

chaos is a confounding destination
uncharted and unbridgeable
subsuming an expected future
revealing the dreamer and the dreamt

in a world of rising sea levels
and voracious viruses
industrial strength concepts
cannot imitate transcendence

stardust

pour in
pure consciousness
veil with stardust
and pond muck

we are part cosmos
part earth slop
undoing ourselves
with rapacious speed
why would we
want to save us?

a splash of ingenuity, yes
but floods of ferocity
fires of venom
maybe worse
disregard toward our
dear earth and its beings

yet I pray for
the hope that waits
at the tar black
bottom of Pandora's box

may stardust
enlighten pond muck
may that box
slam shut returning
our human family to
civility and kindness

may we cherish one another
because of our differences
add back the dove
the olive branch
and most of all
love

threshold

a pantoum in practice

window, door or gate
entrance to another place
a change a shift—fresh start
clean breath new step

entrance to another place
look down, the doorsill beckons
clean breath new step
begin again and yet again

look down, the doorsill beckons
breath will cleanse your heart
begin again and yet again
a new threshold awaits

breath will cleanse your heart
open wide and trust
a new threshold awaits
be brave and take that step

open wide and trust
window, door or gate
be brave and take that step
a change a shift—fresh start

Laura Blatt

Wandering Through the Apocalypse

A simple stroll in the forest
becomes an act of faith
when even the orange sky
begs forgiveness.

On the brink of firestorm,
flood, drought, endless plague
the task is nothing less than
resurrection of sanity.

And as we tend our troubles
redwoods gather water
from mist
from highest canopy.

Far away in Southern spheres
giant Frigate birds still spread their wings
fly thousands of miles
in search of home.

Abby Bogomolny

because I turn on the light switch she thinks I make the sun come out

cats know they are an ornament
for the book on your lap
the clothes on your bed
the page on which you write
they are made to stretch their
claws into your leg

they prefer dumping vases
for water, the algae makes them
more resilient to disease

cats do everything on purpose
if, at first, a meow
is not understood, stronger
measures become necessary.

Abby Bogomolny

Life of the Yenta

the yenta with the big mouth
her timing perfect to interrupt
your thoughts, your sentence
you can't finish a sentence

controls with speech
what she can't control in life
fish she knows, butter she knows
all over the place, the yenta

she's asking you and telling you
with a past in every direction:
saved many little tushies
put them on the boat
away from pogroms
away from ovens
before herself, the yenta
pushed with the mouth
like no man could push with his fist

Abby Bogomolny

Looting

Looting is wrong. I like to take my time when I shop. People who take baseball bats and smash automatic doors allow frantic crowds to rush in and steal dish drainers, towels, electronics, and short shorts. That's no way to shop! I like to compare items. Not all of them are well made, you know. But looters are in such a rush; they stomp through your favorite part of Old Navy to grab poorly-made jeans three sizes too big. And without a sales receipt, they can't be returned for the right size. Half of what they take may end up in the garbage—not the recycling. And not recycling means breaking the law. Let's just face it, Looting is never a relaxing trip. You can't get the right size because mangy people have overturned the displays. It's not satisfying—unless you haven't had fresh water or food for four days because you were waiting for the FEMA in New Orleans. But that's not looting; that's survival.

Angel Booth

Feb 2019

The day you left
I scrubbed out the sink
Washed my hair
Twice Registered for a dance class
Added pink and yellow to my wardrobe
Hid black and grey in the far end of the closet
Put your shirts in a bag for Goodwill
Read forty-two pages of a novel
And slept like a log
Don't you even think of not coming back

Angel Booth

Discreet

A poem is a secret
with one flap
turned down so
you can peer inside
but not know all
A tiny spark of mystery
never fully unclothed
leaving morsels
to melt on the tongue
yet leave you hungry

The Emperor

Stroke of the sword believing
Force is leadership
The heart of a common woman
Held like the grail

The emperor claims it all
The blood red moon
Aries strength
Threat of war
The underground cries of winter

The Empress

The Empress steals the heart
Gently bathes it in the waters of life:
the Nile, the Ganges, the Danube
Two halves
A pomegranate missing six seeds

She hands the halves to the Lovers
Invites them to create
The heart again - whole

Catharine Bramkamp

The Fool

We looked up
A man walking followed
The sun half blocked
By warning + directional signs

He strolled down the one-way street
Defying the prescriptive arrow
Pack on his shoulder

When arrested, he did not recall
A single one of his rights
Are we not all - right?

Every day we step from ordinary
Fragile dreams like teacups
Tossed into a carry-on bag

Catharine Bramkamp

The High Priestess

Adapting to fluid blue circumstances
She spends hours tossing
Bits of pink coral to decorate the sea

A man ventures into the recessive surf
Gathering tiny pink almost living things
Enough for profit in the shops

She changes her mind calls up
A tide that smothers in one gesture
No man while rescuing his bits and plans
Can build up reason against the storm

Catharine Bramkamp

Death

Death releases Judgement

Against the dreams of knights
Release the hanged man release
The victim — but it's too easy

Climbing over and over
Onto the popular cross - I give so much
But no one cares but you must

Discover a singular justice
For yourself and change direction

The unwavering gaze asking you to accept
A sword — a horse
One more chance to roll the dice.

Loving a Sociopath

You said we were eternity,
You a shooting star, a burning mist across the sky
sizzling out long before expected.
I, the full moon,
now hiding behind a cloud,
swallowed into the darkness of who you are.

Marilyn Campbell

Resolutions

There will be no
New Year's resolutions in my house.
Fortified with carbs
my soft belly and
stiff winter joints
need more than
wishful thinking.
I vow not,
make no false promises,
will try only to complete
one sensible task per day
starting with a walk.

I venture out,
begin my morning stroll expand lungs
with cold brisk air, thrust hands
deep into pockets,
count off the steps
until they are city blocks and then miles,
all the while denying
this is anything more than temporary
until it becomes more.

Simona Carini

Walking Along 156th Avenue NE in a City That Is Not at War

I escaped from an air-conditioned office,
from processed cold air
Into the June daylight demanding
sunglasses and granting warmth.

I took off my jacket and scarf, slipped out
of my leather boots, clasped them in my right hand,
stepped onto the runner of grass mowed
to thick-carpet height—along the sidewalk.

The blade tips massaged my soles,
sore after ten hours in leather.
I inhaled warm air, sauntered to my destination.
Luck did not place me in Syria, Yemen or Iraq.
The buildings were intact, the houses roofed,
the grass alive. When I raised my eyes, I saw
a cloudless summer sky, not
airplanes pregnant with bombs.
I indulged in the walk for me and all those
denied.

Simona Carini

Responsibility

Thud
the window vibrated
as if an earthquake
had rattled the house.
The glass intact,
but on the grass
a sparrow
immobile.
I lined a shoe box
with soft fabric
placed the bird in it.
It did not fight.

Thud
a young man
rushed to the ER.
Unvaccinated
unable to breathe
refused care—I read.
The nurses battled him
to keep the oxygen mask.
He tore it away,
they watched
his wings go limp,
immobile.

I buried the bird
in the box,
cried and punched the air.
*Didn't you see the glass
the table, the chair*

behind it?
Not my fault
it's dead
he's dead—
and yet.

Simona Carini

Train Rides from Perugia, Italy

No escape from my mother's stern gaze
or her cigarette's smoke, the train a foreign space
of rigid seats too high for my short legs,
air heavy from too many lungs breathing.
I pressed my forehead to the glass,
watched houses and hills slide past,
dreamed of soaring airplanes, exotic ships, Hawaii.
Nodding to the train's rhythm, I drifted asleep,
woke up as the rail wheels screamed to a halt:
Rieti—nothing there but an aunt's house.

Years later, a train deposited me
to *Milano Centrale*, to my first job, a new life
a long way north of the past. Trains shuttled
me back to my old home for visits.
Sandwiched between bodies, I fell asleep
on a foldable seat, heard words in dialects
I couldn't decode, laced with longing.
People crowded northbound rail cars
clutching their ticket to better pay, shelter, school.
The price, a squeeze of the heart, a lump at their throat
that would thaw when southbound, homebound.
The opposite for me, northbound to freedom
from my parents' conflict. Clanking
covered the memory of their raised voices.

And now I take my seat in the *area silenzio* car,
savor the view in blessed quite: Umbrian hills
greened by vineyards and olive trees
brushed sunflower yellow, gentler Tuscan hills,
Florence station, where I change trains, drink

a creamy *cappuccino* before boarding the *Freccia*.
Long tunnels bore the Apennines. Bologna,
then the Po Valley: fields of greens and browns,
poplars marking boundaries, towns and cities
where we don't stop, bound for Milan or Venice,
still inhaling the oxygen of my own chosen life.

Fran Claggett-Holland

In Times Like These

> *"In Times Like These,*
> *it is necessary to talk about trees."*
>
> — Adrienne Rich

I
In Times Like These

Listen.
      You are overwhelmed.
      You are unprepared.
      You are terrified.
      But open the window.
      Listen to the voices outside.
      They have gathered there.
      Your mothers your daughters
      Your nieces. Your sons.
      Yes, your sons and most
      clear most articulate
      most anguished—
      your sisters.
Put out your hand,
Let yourself be led
Away from the window
      toward the door.

Listen, outside
      you will hear the trees
      you will hear the wind in the aspen
      you will notice the silver undersides
            of the poplar leaves.
Listen to the sounds of these trees.
Listen to Daphne tell of what she learned
            as a laurel tree.

II
Daphne speaks

I once lived among the waters —
the rivers, the springs
a tide pool at the bottom of a waterfall.
My father Peneus, the river god
protected me from lustful Apollo

now my leaves bend to the wind
and I listen to the aspen, the poplar
these trees too have known
the waters of life

in this time of
cosmic upheaval
remember when you
were born of water and
ran with the naiads
along rivers and oceans

when you emerged
from mother earth you
like me were overwhelmed
terrified unprepared
for life without the
cool waters.

Life as a tree
gives stability and
communion
between earth and sky
My leaves change
and fall as I navigate
my world

listen
In these times
imagine possibility
walk the sands that surround you
notice the small

the sea anemone
affixed to rock in its watery home
see how it spreads its tendrils
of pale lapis and deep magenta
shades between those of the artist's palette

step into the tide pool
reclaim the waters of your birth

look to the frog
how it moves
   the gathering in
  the leap
      the landing —
     limbs folded
         silent as stone

Fran Claggett-Holland

Tabula Rasa

Children are no longer taught
to write cursive. That beautiful hand of my father's,
no less impressive when he signed a check
as when he signed his letters and reports.
And my mother's hand, learned the Palmer way,
"move your hand from the elbow," she told me,
demonstrating on the kitchen table.
I could never even approximate her beautiful script
now preserved, along with my father's love letters
in the trunk in my garage.

Letter after letter, back and forth,
they wrote, passionate and private, never imagining
their children would one day sit and read them aloud,
marveling at their youth, their ardor, their
carefully drawn words, their own calligraphy.

A hundred years later, my brother and I,
sitting at the old round oak table,
read in tandem, these words of passion, of love,
of forever, written by these two strangers,
our parents.

Fran Claggett-Holland

adagio cantabile

sometimes memory isn't really memory at all
it starts off that way, but underneath it is
the what-if of your life

you write about the way you played
Beethoven when you were fifteen
but really you

are writing about what if you were still
playing Beethoven, the Pathetique
the second movement

which cast such a spell over everyone
they closed their eyes and came
close to floating

leaving the old upright there
where it stood in the dining room
with you dazed and floating too

and everyone humming the familiar
melody of your childhood
translated into the

reality of your fifteen-year-old self
alone on the stage of every
recital you were ever in

and your mother and father
and brothers and aunts and even
Beethoven himself

smiling as you whisper
is this the way you hear it
now that you are deaf

and he nods and the tears
come and he sits down beside me
and puts his hands over mine

Fran Claggett-Holland

At Death

I

an unbroken egg
the yolk suspended in its ocean

a white curtain fluttering
at the bedside of a child

the milk flowing out of
Vermeer's pitcher

the vermillion of the hummingbird
outside the dining room window

her unlined face a perfect oval
against the enveloping fire opal tapestry

II

on writing the poem
that fell into my fingers

>who is to say
>this word or that

>the word
>always the word

>the words fall
>unpredictably

>Vermeer
>vermillion

who could know to write
them in conjunction

who could know
this was to be

a poem about death
a poem about her death

and about my grandmother's death
all those years ago

a death I never witnessed
but knew

    as she never knew Vermeer
    but knew the hummingbird

    that laid her eggs
    unbroken

    in the tiny nest that appeared
    on the same limb of the same tree

    year after year
    disappearing after the young

    flew into the cerulean sky
    as did she

Fran Claggett-Holland

Until

Your story is not my story.
Your dog is not my dog.
You loved your dog
He was the best dog in your world.
I loved my dog.
He was the best dog in my world.

We grew old.
I had to keep living.
He wouldn't know what to do without me.
I had to keep living so he would keep living.
That's how it was.

Suddenly he grew old faster.
As did I.

One day he just laid down and died.
As did I.

My dog is not your dog.
Still, your story is not my story.

Until it is.

Penelope Anne Cole

Beloved Beauty Mine

She scoots in the door, following the dogs.
She dutifully scratches her post by the door.
Such a good girl you are, I say as I pick her up.

She purrs and snuggles in my hair,
clinging to my neck, kneading me as I need her.

Her warm, lithe body is close and comforting in my arms.
She's limp and strong—a wild beast lies beneath my chin.

I breathe her in.
She smells of sunshine and dirt.
Her fur is sun-warmed and soft,
bunny-soft-fur, once the dirt is off.
I breathe her in again.

Then she's had enough loving for the moment.
She jumps off to check her food dish—then
drink some water—her choice of four bowls.

Surprise! Back again on my desk.
She's settling down behind the laptop.

A short rest or a long nap.
Or a quick lick clean.
Or a leisurely tongue-bath.
Busy pink tongue, perfect pink nose.

She licks the makeup off my face.
At night she sleeps by my head.
She purrs me to sleep
a comfort in the dark room.
Shadows come and go.
She is with me still.

Marlene Cullen

Winter I

Winter is the best time
To look out the window
And watch the weather

Grey clouds float on cat's feet
Storm clouds growl
an angry wolf's warning

And when the rain happens
I stand in the doorway mesmerized
Watching the downpour

Splattering on the asphalt
Soaking into the lawn
Nourishment for the plum tree

And sustenance for me
I inhale a deep breath
I am revived

Marlene Cullen

Winter II

December is a fancy sequined dress
Highlighted with a sparkly necklace
And cherry red stilettos

After the glitz of the holidays
Winter is a refreshing time
For peace and contemplation

January settles around my shoulders
Like a soft, grandmother shawl
Protecting and offering refuge

The warmth of my house on a
Rainy day comforts and soothes
As I gaze onto my yard

From my porch
My eyes scan
The majestic buckeye tree

Her branches delicately
Stretch over the lawn
A summer's canopy

Through her branches
My vision is clear
And far reaching

Joseph Cutler

When Are We Really Together?

Walking out of the night garden
after dancing with ghosts,
we wake, then freshen up
in the bathroom mirror.
We present ourselves
patched together,
Washed, brushed, combed.
We are as present as the lingering vines
of the night garden,
still wrapped around our ankles.
will let us be.

So, when are we really together?
Maybe dancing? But even then
with the voices of the dead
calling out the steps?

We offer kindness, pass the cereal,
pour coffee for each other,
forgive each other for our loneliness.
Maybe it is in this kindness,
this forgiveness of the other's "otherness"
that finally makes the long,
slow walk to the graveyard —
a time to point out to each other
hooded orioles by the creek,
allow sticky monkey flowers
covering the rocks,
fragrant bay trees warming in the afternoon sun.

Joseph Cutler

An Apple a Day

Magritte beat me up in
the parking lot as
I was walking towards my car.
A nicely dressed gentleman-
bowler hat, crisp suit, gold headed cane.
I thought he wanted directions.
He took everything.

Now I know, he's the kind of guy
who will invite you over for coffee
but will slip something into your drink...
without warning you are walking on the bottom
of the deep blue sea,
talking to the glowing pearls
in the giant clams.

Or, suddenly you are flying
over your childhood home,
looking down through the clouds,
an apple for a head,
trying to remember your name.

Joseph Cutler

Crystals

The dark crystals of his
body made sitting anywhere
for very long quite painful. But
as he learned to hold
the dark gems
in his hands,
without tightening-
they would slowly warm and melt,
becoming blood and stories, or sometimes, pictures.

Once or twice,
spirits of people
long gone
would emerge from them,
sing to him and leave.
A few returned,
as feral cats
that he adopted.

Over time, he could cry
more easily, feel people
once invisible to him,
see more colors,
remember his dreams.

Joseph Cutler

Unfinished Business

On his 50th birthday
after the party,
still slightly drunk,
he walked into
a tattoo parlor.

"Let's start with the dog bite
on my calf," he announced,
to the young woman
with a map of Eurasia
stretching from her neck
to her knees.

From now on, I'll say
it was me
that bit the dog!
It came into my yard,
left one mess too many!
I'll say I caught it, bit it
Hard, on the back leg.
That it turned, took a bite out of me.

And the lady next door,
turned a hose on us.
It was a hot day, so
it felt good!
I was done with him
anyway.

So, I want a dog,
with its teeth
dripping blood,
sinking right into that scar.
And I want a little devil
with a pitchfork,
sticking it to that damn dog!

Each scar
became a story. Some true.
Some true in spirit. Some
not even close.
Some were little maps
of places he had never been.
Some, names of women
he had never known.
And, when it was all done,
long after dark, he rejoiced
in his new determination,
to go to all those places,
meet all those women,
and bite all those dogs.

Patrice Deems

Taureans

I
have lost
three
firmly planted
Bulls—
mountain
and
shore
to my sea

I
depended
on their
stable
logic
their
steady
routine
to ground me

where
to
settle
my restless
waters
now?

Paul DeMarco

Larkspur Ferry on the Fourth of July 2021

Half asleep on the ballpark ferry
words bob above swelling murmurs
like the white caps dot the choppy bay.
These are holiday-happy voices,
No sullen commuter silence here.

A thousand people returning
to baseball's secular rituals
like children recovered from a long sickness.
Now we can eat cake.
And ice cream, too!

Through the haze of sleep-wake,
Familiar landmarks long unseen
touch memory, spark odd reflections.
We shrink from San Quentin Prison,
so incongruous in name and jewel setting.

Golden Gate Strait without the bridge lies
just past the imagination, where the fog drifts.
White sails halo Angel Island's lee shore.
Sutro Tower, sky-points lost in low clouds.
I once saw this creature in a misted mirror,
a *fata morgana* of iron spider legs.

Bay Bridge shadow flickers, fast as a bird across the sun.
The Salesforce phallus pokes another disgrace
into the long-ruined skyline.
Coit Tower was the high most building
when I first saw it 50 years ago.

City of light, of promise and delivery,
I join the lament familiar of multitudes
before me who knew you when.

We coast into McCovey Cove,
flow through the keen arches that open
to sharp white lines, impossible green,
cathedral landscape
and 30,000 people, holding this diamond
familiar in timeless common.
Home at last.

Paul DeMarco

The North Star

When ritual bonds fracture;
When handshakes endanger;
When veneer peels, reveals
the sudden care
for the jailed, the homeless,
as mere self-protection;
When our rulers rule clueless,
no skill but deception,
jockeys for advantage
regard-less, care-less,
while their Murdoch*
disgrace the fourth estate;
When factions war
in the uncivil twilight
like fissured siblings
at their father's funeral;

When our economic engine
of consumer consumption
lurches us sputtering
down the bouldered cliff,
while, all out of touch,
mad men at the wheel
scheme to give us
the business as usual,
Hit the gas raving "Go Go Go!"—
that's all that they know—

What will we do?
What will it take, this obscure future
that abruptly demands us?

Where should we start but to find
our own center, deeply in touch,
One by one,   Together.

Murdoch — a Scottish term for describing a man who is a selfish old beast

Paul DeMarco

Transfiguration, Sonoma October

If you watch the ground sprout
with the down of grass
that will rise beyond our reach
before it seeds and slants in May
greener by the hour

if you dance to the first rain's song
hear the streamlet's burble return
revel in the long night sky
Orion climbing sharp-eyed

if you remark the flower pearls of coyote bush
the persimmon tree lantern-draped
clip the fruits by chill moonlight
reverently laying them down
drink the air like a spirit
as it whooshes 'cross the coastal hills
and hums through redwood strains

then you might doubt those
metaphors of death and dying
autumn summons to the poets
punctual as the atomic clock
might question even
your ideas of death itself
and where they came from.

Paul DeMarco

Appropriate Technology

> *"The world begins at a kitchen table."*
> — Joy Harjo, from "Perhaps the World Ends Here"

We build our heroes from scoundrels and fools.
Just as Sisyphus, that nasty schemer
who fractured sacred tradition to feed his greed,
is now the symbol of the nine-to-five workaday grind,
Young Icarus captures imaginations
with a fatal fall from flying too high,
celebrated in paintings and poems
as a lofty attempt to escape the human condition.
Yet, simply put, Icarus fell because
he didn't listen to his dad, Daedalus.
"Don't fly too high, or the sun will melt the wax on your wings."
Seems easy enough.

That brilliant engineer stayed aloft
by minding physics in flight from Crete,
with his son fleeing the wrath of King Minos
for revealing the secret of his labyrinth
to Ariadne and her man Theseus.
No one says why he told her.
He was, I think, as much a fool
in lust as a genius in science.

Was Icarus a tragic hero for the ages?
Or just another teenager wrapping
his Mustang around a tree?
Or maybe Daedalus—
obsessed with his craft,
without moral principle,
jealous killer of his nephew—

wasn't such a good father.
Icarus tuned out his incessant carp,
happened to miss something
in the muddy flood of words.
Maybe they, just like Minos and his queen,
needed a solid kitchen table,
instead of a maze.

We fabricate our heroes
from scoundrels and fools,

Nancy Dougherty

To Escape the Everyday

And all that's missing, gone
to memory, I go to an outdoor café,
find a seat where nearby
a fountain trickles then gushes
gallivanting, fast or slow
expounding, or thundering
fulsome, someone's asking
someone, "What's your sign?"

Farther away,
more white sound, more the
dry backdrop of motorcycles' roar
the swish of Priuses, rush by,
envelope the round tables
grouped under magnolias,
potted succulents,
the umbrellas flared for
sun protection, for the onslaught
of masked patrons.

Night, even further away, the
distance like a diminished
circle towards the black, mind
focusing in, to behold
the scenes of another type of drama,
the inside story of another day
and circumstance, shrouded
by dreamy image. This flash
of night in my day.

Scrape of chairs, the tables
empty, and pigeons hobble off
as if on cue to their eaves. I prepare
too, to leave, wishing for some
clue, some sign to decipher.

Nancy Dougherty

Layers of Love

an artwork by Kathleen Capella

She's made this—this art square 8" x 8"
cut from a much larger rectangle of 4' x 4'—
a canvas stretched, the base upon which
she's glued twenty layers of mementoes,
all sorts of paper over six years' time. Things
like receipts, bills, holiday cards, old love letters,
photographs, the first crayoned strokes
of grandchildren. The trace of fingers,
whole meals, bits of her universe.
An opus to sentiment.

And even the check of red tablecloth, ubiquitous,
that signals picnics and friends and fresh air.
"You surround yourself with uplifting companions,"
the lived epigram, the fortune cookie hovering
in lower left corner. The faces come and go,
daughters-in-law, nieces, mothers, old friends.
Flames flicker over crevasses of expressions
like signposts for the years, and marking
the campsites; Salt Point, Timber Cove,
and further north. Dust devils, sand bits,
the roar of ocean, shells lined up,
crustacean curiosities.

Peel off another layer, imagine the contours
of thoughts, ideas unravel, sword ferns sway.
Impress of hooves among the needles, coolness
of the dawn redwoods. This tablet of recollections
expands in letters, journals, old menus,
snippets of conversing, misplaced diamonds,

the compost for the soul. Hold it close
to your heart, squeeze tightly, it gives a little,
will warm to your touch. And in a quiet place,
bring it to your ears. Listen to the faint heartbeat
of its living pages, scent of rose, grandmother.
Bit of stenciled tee shirt, godchild.

Let's say you make an art square and fill it with
everywhere & everything, what eyes have seen,
where feet have trod—through the Grand Canyon,
Hermit's Rest, Tusayan. Now work it fast,
paste it on—the great heat of that past day
and finish it off, with a thin red ribbon
set diagonal, over the orange streaks
of sunset still so vivid. And flip it over
to the back, to leave your signature
on paper tactile as skin.

Anita Erola

Mourning Doves

after he was gone,
she asked her son
to send her birds,
so she'd know
when he visited

mourning doves appeared

every day,
they arrived
cooing,
pecking around the yard

every day,
she cleared
the kitchen table,
and swept under it

she took the dustpan outside,
tossed the crumbs in the air
and said,
"here birdie, birdie, birdie"

years

she'd grieved
so deep,
so long,

until one day,

enough
the mourning doves
came no more

Anita Erola

The Lemon Cake Dance

the dancers
ready in the wings

butter, soft
eggs, room temperature

sugar and flour, measured
lemon, squeezed and zested

butter and sugar in
bowl spins

both cling to edges
like wall flowers
needing a nudge to join the dance

the prodded
grabbed by pirouetting blades
merge in the round

ease into the two-step
around they go
creamy blend spins
flour, sifted
cascades like ballerina feathers
to join the swirl

eggs
pre-mixed
do the runny slide

last in
lemon zest, a tart twist
and juice, the citrus flair

the velvety batter waltzes
Tales from the Vienna Woods
around in the bowl

the dance stops

the silky blend
glissades into pan
bakes to a golden brown
aroma fills the air

the toothpick, dipped
emerges free
like a modern dancer

ready

to cool down
from the heat

Anita Erola

No. 2085

Every day on my walk, I pass you,
the once majestic oak, with limbs gnarled by time

your bark, like a reptile,
scarred by wind and fire

joints knotted; limbs bent,
like the old man with his cane

acorns dropped long ago, no longer grow

invading wasp nurseries
galls, like Christmas balls, fall

do neighbor trees sense the end of an elder's days
as it's eaten away?

buzzards circle above
a squirrel scurries below

your roots transmit what earthlings do not hear
but I hear you

the Acorn Woodpecker drums

the grand tree stands, still
as if petrified

a metal tag, No. 2085
nailed to its side
its days numbered.
The old man walks on.

Rebecca Evert

Lament

> *"The function of prayer is not to influence God, but rather to change the nature of the one who prays."*
> — Soren Kierkegaard

How do you pray
Who do you pray to
What do you pray for

Questions asked
Answers unknown or unheard
This wondering
This wandering
This labyrinthian life

Wanting to feel each footstep
Leave an imprint on the earth

Left with no choice
Turning again and again

I keep walking

Because at this moment
This is the only way

I know how to pray

Robin Gabbert

Dental Hygiene

I close my eyes because it's better that way.
The light is bright above, and
I know the drill, so to speak.

The hygienist is giving me instructions
which I understand, although they sound
like the parents do in the Peanuts cartoons.

She starts by measuring my gum recession —
Calling out numbers to a colleague: 3.2, 3.3, 2.2
while piercing my gums with a pointy crooked piece of wire

At least that's what's on the one end of the instrument
I can see when I do occasionally open my eyes.
She says my numbers have improved

but I find my hands, clasped together in my lap,
are still unnaturally gripping each other — as if
by some magnetic force, even when I try to relax.

She asks if I'm okay with "the ultrasonic".
"Sure," I say, not quite sure I remember
what that is. Then the sound brings it back.

There is a high-pitched squeaking-squealing
behind a pressure noise, that sounds like a wee mouse is
being tortured with a water cannon. Repeatedly.

Once that is done, we move on to scaling.
I picture a tiny mountain climber on my teeth. That's better, I think.
The reality is a scraping sensation, a garden trowel rubbed over stones.

I try not to think about it that way, instead
I think about fish being scaled on a stainless
steel sink. Somehow, that doesn't help.

Then I'm ready for a polish and I breathe a
sigh of relief, knowing this is the final stretch.
The hygienist sends me home with a daily fluoride rinse

and instructions to return in six months.
I'm already dreading it, so I swear to start
flossing— regularly. And I mean it.

Robin Gabbert

Nose Job

I was the serious big sister.
There for support. You —

Smiling, always smiling,
unworried during pre-op prep.

The wait while you were under dragged on....
I stared at the wallpaper, tongue depressor beige.

Paging through fashion magazines
in the waiting room, I

kept wondering— did you *really* need rhinoplasty?

Yes, your nose was a little
crooked, not unlike mine.

When you came back, you were
not smiling. White gauze bandages

cocooned your face. There was purple
and black swelling where your eyes

had been. The room seemed hot,
the walls melting. Nausea

like morning sickness swept me.
I wasn't pregnant.

Then I was on the floor.
Later I drove you home.

You slept sitting up on the couch.
Your head a thundercloud—

dark shadows with occasional
showers, or rather, leakage.

I slept on the floor beside you
suppressing my own storm.

Robin Gabbert

BPS (Blank Page Syndrome)

I wonder if white might become my new favorite color.
It's the one I see the most, day after day,
the lonely cursor blinking at its edge.

White— the color of snow, pristine, pure,
the color of an egg (well some),
lovely Italian marble, and luminous ghosts.

Perhaps I should be happy to see a blank
page, free from the detritus of my mind.
No evidence of that internal struggle—

the glacial, constipated lack of movement
toward words being typed on a page,
just to be deleted, juggled to and fro, and cursed at.

Just maybe, white
        is the new black.

Robin Gabbert

Posthumous Epithalamion for Ethel & Sid

There once was a girl, eyes bluer than her hair was black.
All shy smile and pearls in the faded Daguerreo,

But she clipped off the extra thumb of a new-born baby
as a nurse trained by old Doc.

Sid broke his arm delivering messages by motorcycle in World War I,
then became a brakeman on the B&O.

He rode the rails for days before returning for doses of
her generous laugh, chicken-and-dumplings,
and nights sitting together on the porch.

The wooden swing creaked, till the children were abed.
Then, following fireflies in the stairway windows,

he'd lead her upstairs quietly.
She, still prone to giggle like a schoolgirl.

Seventh daughter of the same, Ethel had visions, and dreams,
and sometimes knew of undisclosed nightmares,
locations of lost keys, and things still to occur.

Sid later turned gruff as the TB ate his lungs—
afraid to share a sip of coffee with five-year-old me.

But he'd still smile and untie her apron,
when she was least expecting it.

Now, the porch swing of the old house on Gallia Street
is gone. It's someone else's house now,
run to ruin, left to the ghosts.

But blue eyes shine on
in grand and great grandkids
and, day or night, her laugh still infects

all who will remember.

Christina Gleason

Evering

Soundless rifling
the silent pressings
muffle-downed weight
grips
a blunt soundless
frightened fist

but wherever are birds sounds
against the wearied day
when you will not glean
nor gather grace
upon the rifling consignments
opposed to aural sustenance

where is a convocation
to be found
as the fore of this load
accepts no appeal
nor entreaty
to ghosts now?

evering feathers
ever naught
everness of evers
chant upon the endless evers
and their feathering come
earnestly evering …

call the evering
call to the air
call thusly
call trustfully
call them now
call to bird sounds

Joan Goodreau

When Will It End?

The iceberg we're floating on is melting faster than we thought
by flames and ash   red and grey
our molten words   red and grey

Like my mother used to say, "You have been warned."
but we paid no heed until too late
we now make rhymes about polar bears
reminisce about old times.

Together in an elevator permanently out of order
we stand six inches apart   don't speak   eyes straight
    ahead.

Masked strangers
bandits we rob each other for a house with a view
a senate seat   a shopping cart with working wheels   one million
    followers on Instagram.

"When will it end?"

When our iceberg melts away
the way a chunk of ice disappears in the punchbowl
after the guests have gone.

Joan Goodreau

Before and After Spring

Before

My lips press against
silence-swaddled bud, clinging
chrysalis to hold
secret promises to come.

Before the unfolding bloom
of words is space for stillness.

After

Lilac blooms fade rust.
I breathe deep their dust and try
to smell fresh branches
lick rain on petals at night.

Moist and shining in the dark
the caves of our mouths open.

Joan Goodreau

Fire Season in Bidwell Park

the old sycamore cracks a warning
its arthritic limbs will tumble on
the juggler tossing pins
and waves its arm good-bye

its arthritic limbs will tumble on
tai chi mummers dancing
and waves its arm good-bye
our parched charred earth untended

tai chi mummers dancing
the juggler tossing pins
our parched charred earth untended
the old sycamore cracks a warning

Joan Goodreau

Exposed

When my son Ian was three
I waited for his test and diagnosis
of the Spectrum mysterious
wondered where it could come from.

Now forty years later
I wait for his test and diagnosis
of a virus mysterious
wonder where it could come from

worn-out vaccination
times he took his mask off and I'd put it on again
grocery store lines   jam-packed bowling alley   nephew's
    birthday party
day-program picnic   McDonald's woman with a cough

In clear air
not the smoke we choked
from burned-down gold-rush towns
all summer long

in air transparent
invisible globes with flaming crowns.

Joan Goodreau

Vet

My father never sent off for his medals
or saw action-packed WWII movies
or talked about his adventures
with his old army buddies.

My mother collected photos of him
smiling with his troops like his high school football team
sitting on a horse he'd learned to ride English style
while waiting to cross the Channel

letters complaining of cold so bitter
we never went camping like other families did

newspaper clippings of his landing on Normandy.

Sometimes he took old torn maps out of a trunk
traced the lines with his finger across France and Germany
told me he'd ridden on the meat wagons of the wounded
how his tank was a tin can waiting to explode.

"Why did you go? You had a kid and could've stayed to work the
    family farm."
        He looked at me the way he looked at young salesclerks
           in his store
        who can't do sums in their heads, who can't count change
           back.

After reading *Anne Frank* in high school, I asked if he'd seen a
    concentration camp.
        "We were first in Auschwitz.
        Tough. It was tough."

Tramping through conquered lands
no cheering liberated crowds (for him)

only the greeting of skeletons and ghosts not yet dead.

Chlele Gummer

Sept 2020

What's more than this?
A third of our nation burning
Many dead with covid
Life at an unknown edge

People stirring for a fight
Glassy eyed from worry
Wondering what we should be doing
At day's end achieving nothing

Why bother with daytime clothes
Who needs makeup or hair combed
How do I pass the time
Without you who am I?

Orange skies reach the horizon
Red sun rides the clouds
Ashes dusts the patio
Air catches in one's throat

Hiding out from covid
Hiding out from bad air
Hiding out from loneliness
Hiding out a standard awareness

Can one see beyond the minute
Can you plan for the day or not
Can you make a claim on the future
What's more than this?

Karen Hayes

Stones

I first picked stones
at age five or six
for my mother
white quartz glittering
among the rocks piled
near the railroad track
they seemed a small treasure

others skimmed over water
where I could not go
like sticks floating away
to otherness

these past years
I have scrounged many
gathered at the river
ocean beaches
or dug up by boot heel
a little something to distract

among dirt and generic grey are found
reds, stripes, whites, almost blues
mottled, blended colors
and the small almost fist-sized green
looking like a cousin to deep jade

sitting now upon my desk
stones wander
through solitary landscapes
with me

stones keep me occupied
keep me company
they have not yet
weighed me down

Pamela Heck

Warrior with a Walker

I was the watchdog at my mother's gate,
bound by chains forged link by link from love and guilt,
a silent witness to her deep despair.

I sold her car,
watched independence drive away,
packed her life in boxes
to be stored and shipped,
demanded that she trade her world for mine.
California, so many miles from home.

Things were left, but I was right.
Later, she said so too.
Still, it was hard to see my mother cry.

She missed familiar places,
old friends, and seasons most of all.
Such grief, and then—
a renaissance.
She learned to paint,
wrote poetry, made a friend.
Flowers plucked from public places
bloomed again on hand-made cards
bestowed on those in need of care.
Happy Birthday — Please Get Well — In Sympathy — Joyous Noel.

Life took the things Mom cherished most.
It spared just me.

My mother clung to quiet coves
while I preferred the open sea.

I told myself we weren't alike,
and yet...
I do a thousand things like her.
She peeks from every passing mirror,
confronts each unmade bed and unwashed dish,
pats every passing dog and cat.
I learned the worth of simple kindness,
that bravery can be defined
by small victories strung together,
like getting up and getting dressed.
Mom's tenacity lives in me.
I never knew how strong she was—
until the end

Pamela Heck

Coming Storm

A breeze—
playful fragment of impending wind—
tugs my hat and moves on.
In its wake,
leaves scudder, flag flaps.
Storm coming,
Not yet.

Past winds—
harbingers of fire and falling trees—
make me cautious,
but there is no fire today.
Instead, I breathe
fresh scent of coming rain.
A promise.

Storms come.
The sightless eye within each squall
provides a sheltered space,
calm center between
past and future, was and will,
and in that respite,
all is still.

Pamela Heck

Genesis

I believe it more than rumor
that God has a sense of humor,
proven by such mundane facts
as hiccups, sneezes, and earwax.
Between the silly and sublime,
he must have had an awesome time,
designing creatures great and small,
for the glory of it all.
Lost in the solitude of space,
did a smile cross his face
once he'd shaped the blazing sun
so, he could see what he had done?
Did he revel in delight
at the hummingbird's first flight?
When shaping the giraffe,
did he have a little laugh?
Or did he find that neck so fine
that it deserved a lofty line?
Did he think, "I really ought
to give those elephants more thought?"
finding them a bit too baggy
with their skin so loose and saggy.
Is evolution God's correction,
or does he find it all perfection?
And if, like God, I too could see
perfection in a lowly flea,
could I see it, then, in me?

J. L. Henker

Island

Lush symphony of birds
pungent azure breeze
resurrection morning
rich, vibrant

Tender woven
tropical caress
Joy
Alive

Basha Hirschfeld

David loves rocks

David loves rocks
I am mercurial,
perhaps he loves that
in me.
When we first met
we took a trip
to the coast of Maine.
Standing on the jetty by the sea,
he spied a shiny red thing
buried in the grey,
took out his jackknife and said to me
(his new found lover, with him for a spree)
"you're standing in my light."
I should have left him then
appalled and mortified to be
merely an obstacle between
him and his discovery.

How often has it been since then
that he, content amid his rocks,
allows me to wander uselessly about
while he with purpose and with glee
attacks the grey stones, pulls the shiny gems out.

Am I not a gem as well,
is he not aware of me?
"You're in my light," he says
and I, obedient as a mole,
get out of his way
so he can pursue his goal.

I didn't leave, I stayed around
for forty years, I tried to be
the gem in the rock
that he wanted to see.

But I am neither gem nor rock
nor ice nor water, fire or snow
I'm all of these at times
all seasons and all kinds
of weather.
Don't need to be what I am not.

Looking within for the hidden gem
I say to myself
"you're blocking my light,"
and smile to know
there's nothing left to fight.

Basha Hirschfeld

Running through the Rain

His mother left when he was two
How could she?
What did he do
to survive?
Moving target.
Never stop to pause
Never pause to stop
The weight would be too much
Did you know moving slow
Through rain
You get less wet
He said that
But he doesn't
Move slowly
Through anything
And I remain watchful
For the breaks
When will he fall
When will he have to stop
And when will all the rain
He has been running through
Soak him to the bone

Basha Hirschfeld

To My Writing Class

a coven of witches
spin the wool of thoughts
into words

they strip away the veneer to peer
at the core
true carpenters
darkened
blacksmiths hammering away
at the glowing lynchpin of the heart.

My hair like Medusa's on fire, on fire:
Smoke curling up from a smoldering mind.
I pale before the wizard's wand,
go mute as swans' tongues and afraid.
Is it false modesty that slows my hand?
Or can I push through as grass is brave?

I reach into the crevasse of my mind
to find one true word worthy of a life.
I bow to you oh sound of sounds resounding,
A balm to flames of random thoughts and calming.

A friend takes my foot in her hands, I feel
the blood, the breath, the rattling of the chain.

Basha Hirschfeld

boomerang trajectory

I circle back.
eat marijuana chocolates
as if I were in my twenties
trip over my shoes
in the entry hall of awakening.

I follow poetry around like a lapdog,
tongue hanging out, ears drooping,
loyal but not swift. the early eager hope
now slouching in late seasoned doubt.

The tide folds in on itself
the moon pulls at me, I want to
curl up in my mother's lap.
boomerang trajectory

throwing me back on myself.
a human mobius strip.
feeling my way down through
to the source.

the words of a song
first heard
as I crossed the mountains
heading west. "*California
will you take me as I am
will you take me.*"

can we come any closer
to our dreams than this place
yet still we ask the question
will you take me as I am?

I want to crawl up into
the sleeping bag
with my first lover
and start again.

Word by word I weave my tapestry
feeding on poetry and rainbow light.

Jon Jackson

Stars On A Rainy Night

Where do they go,
Those starry stars,
Those winking lights,
Those distant suns,
Lanterns of the night

They fall to earth,
As drops of life,
And flow as streams
To open seas,
Back to the sky.

Mara Johnstone

The Mundane Years

The stories tell us
of time traveling heroes
who send messages to the future
by way of a bank,
or a family of lawyers,
or several generations of postal employees

Those notes always arrive
with a curious messenger
who has a bet going with his compatriots
about what this is all about

He always gets some answers,
though never all of them

What the stories don't tell us
is about those middle generations,
the people who will never live to see
the message delivered
but who also
didn't personally agree
to the stewardship of it

What about them?
What must it be like
to never know?

I wonder if any ever peeked,
a secretive Pandora,
unable to resist

I wonder what it's like
to know that you broke the sacred seal
and STILL don't know what it meant

Mara Johnstone

A Variety of Earthlings

Snakes walk
with their ribs

Some fish have teeth
in their throats

Many deep sea creatures
are red
because it makes them invisible

Some female moles
are only female
in breeding season

Why would I,
sci-fi writer that I am,
need to make anything up
for alien worlds
when all this already exists?

Karl Kadie

Night Muse

You can't escape
the poem that wakes you at night
crying "write me."

If you switch on the light
and record the words,
you may discard it later as drivel,
or you may extract a precious kernel
as if cracking a raw walnut
to find a morsel shaped like your brain
that tastes so sweet, so carefully spiced,
you dream about it for years.

If you don't write it down,
if you shrug your shoulders
& drift back to sleep,
the poem disappears
like a lone dog bark on a distant block,
and you forgo,
perhaps forever,
the treasure of night poems
strung together over time
into a necklace of truth.

Karl Kadie

Grace

Tom wishes this day never happened.
Smoke meanders down streets
like unwanted, dangerous dogs
exploring the buildings with food left outside.
He stares at the hills a few miles away,
where flames shimmer red through gray gauze
like a distant Fourth of July.
Though he leaves with evacuation notice in hand,
he is confident South Lake Tahoe
will escape the blaze.
He learns from the Internet
the Caldor fire is partially contained,
traveling east on the Pioneer Trail,
not north toward the lake and his home.

On Highway 50 past Zephyr Cove,
traffic bunches like an angry mob
but Tom is not perturbed, only relieved.
Truck windows seal his eyes and nose from smoke,
soul music on the radio soothes, and
his wife's voice on the telephone reassures.
He knows the outcome could be worse:
his old green truck might cough
to a stranded stop in the dirty, disaster air;
or he could stay and test the notice
while the dark light of night
bursts through his doors and makes Tom
the final note in an out-of-control symphony.

Tom reminds himself God does not
give out lucky cards to everyone.
In a few hours he'll arrive safely in Aptos.
He can relish in his wife's upbeat discoveries
from her canvassing of their coastal town.
He can eat grilled salmon with the cool whisper
of chardonnay trickling down his throat.
After dinner, he might turn on music,
listening to the bow of dreams
slide over the violin strings
toward a melody he's never heard before.

Anne Keck

Victoriana Apologizes

Apologies

I, Victoriana, youngest dragon of the Mirror Fold and first in the Line of Ascension, Daughter of Beatrice the Wise and Magmar the Great, Apologize to all my human friends and neighbors who have lost pets in the last two weeks. They were delicious.

Apologies, Again

I, Victoriana, the current leader in the Wings Around the World competition, Have been informed that my recent apology was not as sensitive as it should have been. I humbly ask your forgiveness and, if it is any comfort, inform you that The cats in particular were far too hairy and not as scrumptious as they could have been.

Apologies, Thrice

I, Victoriana, hereby give notice that I have promised to attend cultural awareness training And to watch what I eat and how I talk about my prey, I mean, diet And to use the privileges I have been given and my own innate talents to help others. Even if it means my snacks from this point on will be boring.

Briahn Kelly-Brennan

All Along The Serious Day

Moods moving like clouds
or wanderings of the unplanted
Sun floats in its shell of sky
five naked ladies
turn pink at the sight
despite the urgent explanation of the leaves

When four frogs under an upturned bucket sing "La Donna E
    Mobile"
a rabbit in a black leather jacket will enter your dreams
and we will drink a book a day
as sylvan sounds
rub the bowl of your ear
until it rings
until it sings
until it opens

Briahn Kelly-Brennan

Slow Drift of an Untethered Mind on a Sunny Afternoon

A thought appears
A sudden memory
Some shooting star
Extinguishing all others

A memory
Its randomness
Extinguishing all others
Your face in profile

Its randomness
That small telling gesture
Your face
As I knew it

That small telling gesture
Unconscious in its revelations
I knew it
Something passed between us

In its revelations
Something was understood, settled
Passed between us
Though really nothing happened

Something was settled
As if nothing happened
And really nothing happened
But what was that

As if nothing
Some shooting thought
But what is that
A star appears

Crissi Langwell

Wolf Howl

His wolf howl startled me
as I lay on the tangerine floor
covered in scrapes and stones
while my mother dabbed my wounds.

He swore he'd sell that damn truck,
the one with the gelatin seats and shoestring locks,
and the lack of seatbelts that allowed a little girl
to soar through the air,
then watch from the gravel
as her dad drove away.

I didn't understand his tears
as my little body quivered
on the sterile hospital table,
shaking from the Popsicle metal
and the drumbeat of my skin
as they picked rocks from my face and knees
and offered ocean wave whispers among my jellyfish cries.

I was confused by his promise
that he'd never drive that truck again,
and figured it was hard to give the buyer the keys,
saying goodbye to the classic white trophy
he'd cherished forever,
or at least since before I was born.

But the day my womb emptied,
my aching arms never filled,
a wolf cry in my lungs,
and my glass heart shattered,
I knew he'd give away the moon
if it meant
his child would be safe
forever.

Shawn Langwell

Spring

Spring is a magnificent season
where buds form on barren branches,
and new growth pokes its head out like a bear
from the hibernation of winter;

where the fragrant aroma of plum blossoms
and life-giving buzz of bees remind us of
the grandness of nature and all that it is and was.

Where new ideas spring forth
emerging like a Monarch from a chrysalis,
ready to flit and feed on nectar bearing flowers,
because that's what they do.

Spring and fall are my favorites season's by far.
Just the right amount of light in the day
to get some stuff done in the yard.

Just right, spring is
like the tale of "Goldilocks and the Three Bears."
Three cheers for more light and longer days
because spring will soon be here.

Three cheers for new tales spun
like a spring spider's web waiting
for more readers to linger awhile longer,

like the monarch on my knee, where
it rests for a moment before
before fluttering off.

Betty Les

Trees and Other Friends

Ancient oak
canopy still full
and round
twisting twirling branches
adorned with mosses and ferns
come alive with the rains
it is my first stop

the eucalyptus next
trunk spilling out
over concrete
like elephant feet
on trodden path
its immense presence
soothing me
like a psalm
I cross the street

to a whole block
of ginkgoes
branches obscured
by mango-colored leaves
ambering the air
mellowing my senses
I linger, move on

to the walnuts
stately in their senescence
limbs lost
trunks riddled with holes
home to bluebirds come spring
I bow in reverence
turn homeward

toward the magnolia
exuding grace
sheltering the big
red house on the corner
a neighbor, my friend
standing there
looking up
as I do
drawing her hands
to her heart

Betty Les

Last Stand

> *Sequoia National Forest*
> *California Wildfires, 2021*

What do they
make of us
after all that has
come and gone
these thousands
of years
hosing down
the forest floor
frantically clearing
vegetation
wrapping their boles
in a blanket of foil
encircling them
if necessary
with our own
exhausted bodies
a last stand
between the trees
and the fires
while others
who do not
hear their song
pump out
choking gases
killing them slowly
but just as surely
as the flames

Betty Les

The Stirring

I felt it this morning
somewhere between
brain and bones
a deep stirring
there was a certain quality
to the light
scent to the air
suddenly, urgently
I needed to
shed my cloak
go outside among
flowers set to blossom
trees set to green
birds coming into color
the fresh earth
awakening
a chrysalis
splitting open

Betty Les

Holy Water

Sierra Nevada

Snow
melting on
mountain tops
awakening fingers
of precious water
flowing down, down
into the big rivers
into fissures
and cracks
to aquifers and wells
plumbed into my house
my shower
anointing my skin
my parched spirit
with holy water

Betty Les

Rain Sharpens Memory

I sit at my desk
learning left from right
it is my first day of school

rain slaps the windows
the sky dark as night
I whisper over

and over
flag on my left
door on my right

knowing already
I had no innate
sense of direction

I transferred to the big
public school next year
the youngest kid in the class

it rained that first day too
no thunder and lightning
just drizzle

against a steel gray sky
the classroom dimly lit
by globes

suspended from a high ceiling
I searched for
something anything

to anchor me
there were no desks
only tables

no flag
no door beside me
no welcoming smile

too young
too lost
to look within

Sherrie Lovler

Persimmons

I wonder if they wait every year,
like I do,
for persimmons to ripen.
Today the Cedar Waxwings found my tree.

For them I left all the fruit
that touched the sky.
Maybe they waited for the first frost,
for that delicate mushy sweetness.

Now I watch
as they fly back and forth,
their neat gray feathers
tipped with red.

Through all the worries of this and that,
illness and despair,
the birds still come
and feast.

Sherrie Lovler

Ode to Nightshade, My Cat

Long after you are gone,
I will still feel you in the morning
walking on my body,
pawing my face.

Long after you are gone,
I will sweep up a hair—
remnants of lost love,
maybe even find a whisker.

Long after you are gone,
every pair of dark shoes
seen from the corner of my eye will
catch me off-guard
with a glimpse of you.

Oh, how I dreamt
if a cat came to my door
I would keep her.
Then you, abandoned in the field,
were brought to me by a friend.

All of seven weeks old,
you sat in the palm of my hand,
then on my modem,
then on my printer,
and every warm place you could find.

Playful, endearing,
your long brown hair and yellow eyes
rendered you beautiful.

Your skittish nature
kept you from others.
You were mine, all mine to enjoy,
and I did completely.

Now, I watch every breath,
every precious moment—
waiting for my heart to be torn
from my body,
reliving 18 years of joy.

Oh, my little girl, I bid you sweet farewell
as I brace myself for that last gasp of air,
the breaking of earthly bonds
that animals bring to the human soul,
the love that cannot be expressed,
only known.

Sherrie Lovler

Grove Street Is Less of a Grove Today

The new neighbors,
with barking dogs and flying flag,
nary a smile or hello,
whom I silently praised
for keeping the street clean,
sweeping up the pink petals
from the three magnificent trees
in front of their house,
did what I thought
was unthinkable.

At first it looked like
the trimmers were
trimming the trees,
but the flowers were in full bloom
and it wasn't the right time of year.
Then I overheard,
"We had to get a permit."

My heart sank,
my stomach ached. No!
Not a protest to be seen;
the sleepy neighborhood
never said a word.
I watched as beauty was arrested,
cured, as if it had no place
in the world.

The first tree went down,
then the next,
limb by limb, leaf by leaf,
flower by beautiful flower.

Truck full, the cutters gone.
Dare I pray
for the remaining tree's life?
By noon it, too, was killed.

Now a solemn emptiness hovers
as I look out my window,
the whole street in clear view.
One neighbor I called said,
"People do what they want to do…"
And so, Grove Street
is less of a grove today.

Sherrie Lovler

Brothers

You played,
then hated.

You saw yourself in his actions,
the parts you didn't want to see.

You blamed him
for your faults.

You blamed him
for sharing the same scars.

You blamed him for having
the same mother and father as you.

And inexplicably,
when the tumor arose,
you cried, too.

Sherrie Lovler

Everything New

Everything new starts on a gray day—
the day you want to climb out of, leave.
We create the new
from the old, the tired, the sick.
We create out of longing.

From nourishing our inwardness
new ways appear.
From the depths of winter comes spring.
From the hidden seed—
staggering beauty.

Roger Lubeck

Tenderloin

The Tenderloin, San Francisco's soft under belly.
Wedged between Geary and Market.
Bordered by Powell and Van Ness.
Needles litter the parks, urine and feces mark the streets.
Glaring anti-crime lights expose the city's bowels at night.
The head and the heart of the city are safe elsewhere.

Staying on Nob Hill? Shopping at Union Square?
Come for a look, poverty, drugs, and sex on display.
Remember, park at your own risk.
Crime and death are everywhere.
Keep your head down and avoid the man shouting on the corner.
See life on the edge but put away your cell and hide your purse.

Drug free zones, crowded with street corner entrepreneurs.
Selling coke and meth, Oxy and spice, all organic.
Graffiti on the walls, colorful reminders of the human spirit
Messages on the pavement.
Gang sign or street art?
"Taylor Marie, please come back home, we love you!" written in chalk.

The hungry stand in lines wrapped around a block, waiting for a meal.
Wednesday at Saint Anthony is Chef's Choice.
Make room for the woman in the wheelchair. A man pushes her.
She holds a lifetime of memories in a blue plastic bucket on her lap.
She has no teeth.
What happened to her feet?

A man carries a backpack overflowing with unwashed clothes.
His stained sleeping bag held together with twine.
He sways back and forth holding a single serving.
Nite Cap, Brown Jug, and Lefty O'Doul's define his world.
Shirtless and shoeless.
Without a referral he will sleep on the street.

Two thousand homeless, twenty thousand Single Room Occupants.
What magnet drew them here?
Camping in doorways, laid out on streets.
Was it desperation and despair that took the light from their eyes?
Did the drugs and alcohol chisel the youth from their faces?
Covered in grime, the sidewalks lights no longer illuminate a way out.

Steven Lubliner

Mudder

You stumbled on the firm fast track. The slop,
The troubled path was home. You cleared the way
So others could run fast. And then you stopped
And let the world pass by and lost the day.

If you had found the strength to throw your mount
And not let circumstance become the whip,
Then better days too numerous to count
Would follow as you captained your own ship.

In freedom, you were horse and rider, too.
You took the bit; the reins your hands held fast,
I tried, but there was no convincing you
To leave the muddy track where you came last.

Torn tickets strew your grave. No new beginning.
You bet against yourself and lost by winning.

Steven Lubliner

Fodder

If there's an afterlife and I wind up
Where you are, as I will, you'll call my name
And chase me with your chess board and your cup
Of hot black tea and ask to play a game.

If you are at your best, which will depend
On where we are, you'll beat me in a walk.
In chess, I'm prone to failing to defend.
In life as well. But . . . now we'll finally talk.

A man's life lived, I still would get to be
That wounded boy, with hurts still raw, in pain.
When every year or so, a memory
Intrudes, I'll ask, "Dad. What the hell? Explain."

And so the time will pass quite easily.
Til others come and ask the same of me.

Marianne Lyon

Starlings

A black swarm
takes over evening sky
wheeling and whooshing
and suddenly

they are dancers
pirouetting unpredictable
in frigid breeze
over Jefferson pines

On this starlit backdrop
bright moon
catches their flutter
like ebon constellations

expanding then closing
and I watch this visual duet
of stars and star-birds
magnificent and fragile

as a single blink.
How did this communion happen
with no communication
no planned meet up

only a stepping out
onto the night sky stage
tonight, maybe again tomorrow
iridescence their common song

I feel my legs lift me
my arms begin to swim
sinking and rising,
I bid my feet to jump me off this

winter ground over scented branches
I want to fly into dazzling performance
I want to see full moon's grin close up;
hear wild cackle of applause.

Marianne Lyon

You think I am lost

"When creation was a new and all the stars shone in their first splendor,
'Oh the picture of perfection.'
But one cried of a sudden
'It seems that somewhere there is a break in the chain of light
And one of the stars has been lost.'"

— Poem by Rabindranath Tagore

You think I am lost
so you shut your strife-charred eyes
to night's radiant lashes

so you forget how to listen
hum undertaker's tunes

You think I am lost
so you linger on barren grave
of your dreams

so you weep,
blind to holy water
leaking from your swollen eyes

You think I am lost
so you miss an arrow
of geese catching the moon

so you whimper awake
wait for sleep to return

You think I am lost
so sleepless, you churn out
long faced poems,
forget that starry verses compose themselves

so you forget to keep remembering
how badly you want to see

Marianne Lyon

I look at you

looking at nocturne sky
light drenches your face
radiant like a pearl
your eyes dart
connect celestial diamonds
your head swings
savors vast montage
of gathering constellations

Your lips part enough
for a silent "aah"
send a gentle glance
for a long moment
then return radiant eyes
to celestial epic
utterances are hidden
under a bushel basket

So different yet
We are caught up
held in this single
emotion of wonder

I wish I could climb
into your skin
watch from your eyes
know if you
are a mute coyote
disguised
unleashed
untamed

miming a howl
at full moon

Wish you could see
through my eyes
a wilderness sanctuary
stars flickering like votive candles
my innocent choir girl gaze
ascending to sacred
glittering sacraments

Elaine Maikovska

Time

We keep decorating rooms
We no longer use
The outdoor table where we never sit
needs a new umbrella,
green with white stripes.
Trying to preserve what once was
Our rooms 3-D pages in albums of closed decades
Memories ensconced in objects
Brass wedding gift candlesticks, their metal tarnished
From hands touching so many times to light a dinner candle
The light glistening
in my children's eyes
If my kids get these in the future
Their kids will doubtless say
How pretty is the Light
the candles cast our way.

Catherine Montague

In the Aquarium

Have you no sense
I tried to ask them
the other evening when
they were trying to leap out
of our aquarium
and gasp infectious air

Why do you always
jump the gun I asked
is it because you doubt
the scientific experts or maybe
it's hero worship for those
self-destructive warriors
who think they can resist
even the deadliest plague

Speaking for myself
one swimmer answered
we've grown weary of routines
and look for excitement
safety feels like captivity
and it seems unlikely that
today's peril can claim us all
some of us might make it

When I think of happiness
outside these walls
even if it kills me
better than a long life
swimming around bored
why not take the chance

and see what happens
and so we leap—

That's what freedom means
it is better to show courage
even for an instant
and then fail
than to swim in circles
and never know which of us
is the one in a million
who can beat the odds

Before I could object
to this feral philosophy
the other swimmer leapt out
disappearing into hostile air
landing somewhere unknown
I never saw the point
for myself I'd rather have
less courage and a longer lifespan

I keep swimming around
waiting for someone to tell me it's safe
but at the same time I wish
there was something I was
as certain about as that
swimmer who jumped out

Rod Morgan

Coastline

The morning mist was full of strangeness, an oddness in the air.
An albatross unfurled his wings and drifted upward on the current
as the gale careened off the headland cliffs. The sea floor quivered,
rumbled and snapped with a lurch. The angry sea rebuked the
   lunar tug,
launched a tsunami that surged and washed the land. The earth
   shuttered
and shook with aftershocks, then rested to wait another hundred
   years.

Jennie Orvino

Nature Walk with Simone Whitecloud

The naturalist, jewel in her nose glinting like a daylight star,
climbs from the creek bed, ecstatic, with a just-emerged caddisfly
on her fingertip. I observe the milky-winged new adult
through the eyes of a micro glass. "It's dazed," she says, "from leaving
its exoskeleton behind." A one-month life. "Unless it meets a
  windshield."

Eye to the pluck line of this glacier-carved valley
I stand on asphalt, once the basin of an ancient lake,
wondering how one needle of the lodgepole pine could be home to
40 kinds of fungus, and another needle another 40.
The Sierra Nevada, snowy mountains, are offspring of under-earth
couplings, granite and lava rock rise opposite, separated by
waters gathered in the cleft. Creeks meandered for centuries
until non-native condos invaded.

If the tiny chickadee must eat every 47 seconds all day and night,
and blackbirds muscle their redwing plumage into hiding
just to survive one alpine winter, who am I to grumble and fret,
hungry for lunch, distracted in so many ways?

If *Pinus contorta*—that amazing lodgepole—grows one cone
for fair-weather conifer sex, and one cone that springs to seed
only in the heat of forest fire, why can't I,
thin-barked, short-lived creature that I am, adapt?

Jennie Orvino

For the memorial

A tall woman writes a vision of her passing:

Redwood topples into waiting arms of the surrounding grove
is held, like bow to cello, suspended. An indelicate wind
rubs her deeply-grooved bark against the bark of her kin,
a keening song.

A hummingbird of a woman wants to hurry death along:

she enjoys eye-candy of this world, but is weary,
at last sinking into her own shadow. She strokes
the eyebrows, the downy cheeks of her visitor
who kisses the oh-so-thin forearm, skin transparent
as a Cosmos petal. They repeat to each other *I love you,
I love you, goodbye.*

Those left behind—she who plays cello, she who sings—
face a morning when the clouds do not break.
Their tribe gathers to roll aside one boulder of grief
after another. Nothing else to be done. All of us, in our way,
are waiting to fly.

Jennie Orvino

If I found a sweetheart

If I found a sweetheart this year, we'd be in the honeymoon phase
until I turned 80, and when the 7-year itch arrived, I'd be 83,
and chances are when I hit 86—the age predicted I would die
by Swami Hariharanda in my yoga horoscope—
we'd be contemplating splitting up anyway.

I'm thinking of adding to my dating profile:
Healthy 75-year-old with realistic attitude about the long term.
With me you won't have a golden anniversary, but
the honeymoon phase will be amazing
and include the best sex you've ever had.

If I found a sweetheart by Valentine's Day, Easter, or the 4th of July,
when my next cake and candles rolled around,
I'd have a cutie on my arm. And if the plague has passed,
we could take a trip to Italy's Amalfi Coast.

What a great thing to have a mutually passionate pact
to love, honor, respect and communicate in truth.
I know it will be crazy, with worlds colliding, fire, flood,
discouragement and growing pains...
but I'm in, I'm in for all of it.

Jennie Orvino

A Cockatiel Named for Wolfgang Amadeus Mozart

"Wolfie" was raised in a kitchen and imitates to perfection
the beep of a microwave. Also in his repertoire, the first five notes
of *Don Giovanni*. The cockatiel's new owner, a yellow-haired
    14-year-old,
plans to teach his pet to wolf-whistle in anticipation of future dates.

In my dream last night, that innocent bird flew pane to pane,
squawking, flapping and fluffing out—mad and mean as a stray
    bullet.
Flattening then flaring his chartreuse crown, he leapt to my cheek,
clung there by beak and claw the same fierce way he navigates his bars

to scrape the cuttlebone, and whispered in my ear. I woke without
    exact
remembering, but something in the way he grabbed me...spoke of
    missing
the moon's face, of no longer owning the sky. Trapped and voiceless
under the nighttime tarp shrouding his cage, the bird became a
    hooded prisoner

at Guantanamo, cuffed and squatting in a six by six-foot cell, wearing
tropical orange as brilliant as the cockatiel's green-and-yellow breast.

Amy Pane

Birthday 2014

And the grey slips into my hair
like the whisper of summer on the spring green hillside
from the top and into the shade of the valleys
and the year slips past
with the hint of winter chill on a late summer breeze
far off still, yet
beginning to weave itself into the color of my hair
the lines on my face
the weight of my body

I can feel the layers of time
as I flip through the pages of my life
the weight of one experience upon another
I can never go back
I can only look in that direction
as each point slips into the distance
becoming another landmark
in the terrain of my history

I am beginning to understand
how moments pass in this way
in eons and epochs
one era pressing into the next
until the years are piled one atop the other
creating layers like the grand canyon
carved by time and water and weight

It is natural for some lifetimes to crumble
under the gravity
of the one that came before
for some time-frames to compost

to feed the next season of my life
some histories remain
like well preserved monuments
others disappear into dust
leaving scarcely a shadow

Amy Pane

Reflections

She turned around
and caught her reflection
in the words she was writing
she was troubled
by the images
parts of herself she wasn't ready to see
still they came streaming out of the tips of her fingers
words
like little slivers of glass
smiling up at her from the page

Fragments of herself kept flowing out
making silver rivers of moonlight
tiny galaxies
dark forests
the metaphors of her youth
the pent up sludge of
things she had never said
out loud

Her words began to chatter and wail
giggle and cry
she became stuck to the paper
by her own stream of consciousness
until
every last bit of her was represented
in the shiny mirror
of a word
or a sentence
or a story

Amy Pane

Exhaustion

I am a cavernous void
wrapped in the skin of an earthly being

Planets revolve in my head
there are supernovas in my heart
shooting stars run rampant through my veins
lightning and earthquakes, volcanos erupt
new earth forms and breaks off into my depthless oceans
elements chase each other from muscle to tendon to ligament
there is too much space inside I cannot connect to this energy

My frequency is low
a dying sun
illumination fading

trying to run,
my legs give out
I fall hard

Even in stillness, galaxies go on colliding inside me
I stop but do not rest
held here by the sounds in my mind

When I find my still point, it is at the center of chaos
in the eye of my own storm there is silence
and no room for thought or comfort
only the long exhale
and the moment of peace that comes before
the inhale

Amy Pane

Dance for 2020

Dance until your bones rattle
wave your arms
shake your head and shout it out
please,
fill this expanse of silence and stillness
with noise and movement
lift it up until it is joy

Let loose the hysteria
move with the blender of information
whirling around and around
try to look over your shoulder
at what is happening
over there
and over there and over there...

Throw back your head and dance
like the ridiculous clown show this reality has become
this blur of sorrow and gratitude, want and abundance
we have been still for so long our bones yearn to rattle

Like the jack-in-the-box, we stayed in the dark
while the handle turned so slowly
we could not hear the melody
and now the lid has popped off
the world has sprung out in madness

Dance, because the dangers are still present
keep moving, jumping, leaping, yelling,
breath mingling in mantra and song
we have been apart for far too long

stretched far too thin
we can see now how we are bound together

How a flame and the wind can combine to ignite the world

Change comes swiftly and you can dance with the tide
or try to duck out of the way
even flat on the ground you will feel the earth dancing
shaking her shoulders free
the shackles will be melted in the furnace
and used to decorate our new cities

Dance, shoulder to shoulder, smiling behind masks
we will find out together what the next verse will be
more than ever, we are in the same story and
breath by breath
the song will travel around the world

All of time will hear the echo

Linda Loveland Reid

Vortex of Me

I'll never know what it's like to be an angel said, Gabriel
delivering the news to Mary,
to see her expression, of what   delight? Anxiety?
We are in the realm
of miracles.

Angels are cherubs or are they fairies?
I have a friend, a robust poet/artist of a man
who captured fairies in Ireland in a beautiful small box.
Bought them home to Sebastopol.
Really?
How wonderful.

I will not go down into a vortex, that blue-deep space
where my spirit guide might dwell.
My sister's guide is a bear.
A friend has six vortexes in her backyard.
There are shamans and drumming.
Another dimension.
Maybe.

Am I so utterly filled that there is no need to go beyond,
to let in more life?
A heart sated with family, husbands, art.
Do I not already hunt down the next challenge?
Is that enough
to prove worthiness?

Are others more "*woke*" my sister more in-tune?
They call it *speciation*, that moment of crossing
the evolutionary threshold.

Finding the human spectrum that is latent
(they say),
inside us.

I'm not likely to step to the right of my left-brain hemisphere.
Not once have I allowed my fortune to be told,
my life pronounced by another.
I mean, what does 'more life' look like?
More stuff, more commitments?
More joy.

I'll never be many things.
But I've come to grips with
the cacophony that makes up me.
For better or worse,
I am my own spirit.
That other door is closed.
And yet —

Jane Rinaldi

Winter Blues

The blues of winter may happen in an instant:
the smoky blue of dull winter
the blue gray of early morning hoarfrost,
blue hair beneath a sodden hat,
blue gray breath mixing with
the blue brown of car exhaust
may momentarily outshout the exhilarating blue of sky.

Winter blue reflects in gray, rain slick puddles;
noses and lips blue from freezing rain
and blue-veined hands clutch at a hood.
Blue, throbbing, frozen fingers
are shoved into pockets.
Yet, sometimes, a stranger's sparkling blue eyes
can outmaneuver the gray of the day.

Margaret Rooney

Intonations

there are voices beneath my voice
can you hear them?
the little girl in the orchard
listening to light falling through trees

the mother's voice
high false broken over rocks
whispering I'm fine, I'm fine
the satin of her dress like petals
torn from their thorns

can you hear the coyote's howl?
sound from the center
hurled through the throat
flies towards the bright bulb
of borrowed light

listen
these are echoes
in my song

remembered
like a scent
or an old secret

Margaret Rooney

Parrhesia

(speaking candidly)

what is the undervoice of the poet;
silt of the unconscious stirred, sifted
lifted into blue awareness
every mote lit unshadowed
unpinned
like a moth or butterfly set free

it's navigating cracked ice
on a dark river
edges and curves slip under you
like swiveling eels cold-eyed and unavailing
you struggle to stay aloft
to let the current take you

or you are begloomed, weighted down
with dense furnishings, scrolled carpets
heavy lamps giving scant light
in twilit space
where folds of petals the size of bent fingers
fall on the floor unremarked

sometimes thought circles the room
breaks through the ceiling, contemplates stars,
cogitates the moon
sometimes birds speak Greek
hills are like toads moving across the horizon
and palm trees heave their shadows upon the wall

if you're lucky, though
it can be like skipping

over the sea in a swift skiff
quick fluent images come

rapid in the mind
carried on the breath
made visible on the page

overall though
writing looks remarkably
like doing nothing

Margaret Rooney

Nights These Days

expatriated from the warm center of things
under a sky of querulous birds
I walk along a trail of bare winter trees

darkness slowly fills the space
between branches
the pale eye of the moon rises

I think of a time when the door
of night was open to me
I could look up into an unbreakable expanse
my sister in the grass beside me

naming our childhood constellations:
Star Tipped Wand, Princess's Footstool
Seven Magic Stones, Queen's Flashing Ruby

"no, no " Mama says "that's Polaris,
Ursa Major, Pleiades, Betelgeuse
and you forgot the Big Shopping Cart"-she smiles-

I remember how quiet the earth was when
we were young, even quieter before we came
how clean the sky and bright the sun

we could hear the local geese loud and near
as they flew white bellied over the house
blue sky in their beaks
the meadow lark sang us awake

three lifting notes from the fencepost
we heard the mewling of new kittens
in the hay felt them all feathers and pins
their heartbeats rapid in our palms

we knew the whole world was ours
we could name it

Margaret Rooney

Somedays the World is Too Rich to be Eaten

Patricia Highsmith Her Journals

lilies their tongues of light
float in curved bells
sound their white breath
in sky of uncanny blue

sunlight sprawls
over everything
claims objects to gild
rouse or illuminate
speaks in canticles of color

scent lays over the scene like vapor
carnations smell of cloves
peonies of sweet peppers
honeysuckle is the open
window of summer

in this green hour
all the unraveled beauty
brushes my face
like the wet kiss
of a soft wave

a pact has been made
with creation
all the colors
are cradled in truth

it's an arrow in the heart
to know how temporary I am
how short a time I have
to see all that is here
in the little garden of my life

I will ask only small questions today
the world is too big and bright for anything else

Margaret Rooney

That Far Thing So Near

day falls around me
a colorful quilt warm
with ladders of light in trees
plaids of shadow under flowers

air is yellow with pine pollen
I'm gazing through something like gauze
a thin membrane softens shapes
like an old photo or memory

I'm swimming in a sleeve of time
through an ocean of sensation
my mind slippery as a fish

is it odd then that you
should occur to me now
not intrude upon my reverie
but be my reverie

your stance loose and easy
like a young goddess
in the long ago ripe wheat
all the golden acres unfolding

the jacket you wore
still in the closet
holds the shape of your arms

how can you not be here, too.

I know how the fields go on
they are of earth and earth endures

we, though, are like the butterflies of summer
and I have outlasted your time.

Janice Rowley

Themes

Themes weave through my patchwork quilt
Life like woolen strands,
Some, soft as yellow pansies
Glimpsed through rain-spatters
Puddled and misshapen by the wet
Only glimpsed now and then.

Some, flicks of pavonine quickness
Shoot through moodiness
Unprepared or too slow to grasp
Leaving shadows on the psyche.

Others, gaudy as a reveler at Mardi gras
Loud and slow with the booze and music
Easy to catch and discard.
They do return, of course.

Others a mix of vivid and faded
Like an English garden between seasons
Resisting the break of spring.
Blues, lavenders and greens.
These thread through my soul
And hold me hostage.

Dimitri Rusov-Morningstar

Meditation

My heart Is heavy
My mind fills fast with thoughts
That pound pitiless against my heart
Seeking eternal freedom
Just as the sea
Filled to over-flowing
Pounds relentlessly
Unceasing
In it's inevitable conquest
Of the mainland.
Ah   the children of mother nature
Forever pursuing precious freedom
And my heart is heavy
Yet   there is a time
When the surf trickles back again
Once more becoming a part
Of its eternity
Finding peace
In its very being
Suddenly
It is quiet
As the joys of living
And the joys of loving
Release the heavy burdens
Of the heart
Of my heart
And I am free
Once again.

Kathleen Scavone

Blossom Fall

Blossom fall
Nature's beautiful,
Tragic metamorphosis
Exquisite, ephemeral beauty
Holds a mirror to our lives

Kathleen Scavone

Clouds

Morning's silvery pages
Shimmer and glow in first light
As though in competition
To replace sparkling star-light
Now, streaks of pink and purple
Paint the sky
Striated cirrus stirring emotions:
Love
Wonder
Gratitude for yet another day

Florentia Scott

Saint-Michel d'Aiguilhe

Michel, patron of high places,
please help me up Purgatory mountain,
one step at a time
backsliding on icy snow
slickened by other travelers.
My feet slip
on greasy clay revealed by so many others passing.

No more firm soil, no more grass.

The mountain trembles in its long, uneasy sleep.

The damned grow weary of confinement.
Stone columns sway.
The old god stirs, hidden too long in plain sight,
throws off the bloodied robe and crown of thorns,
prepares his ascent.

Can I reach the summit in time, Michel?

But who's side were you ever really on?

And where will I go from the crumbling summit
of this now unsteady peak?

Scott Sherman

Crowned by the Corona

Boomers drop like flies
Senior Centers become Youth Centers
The Great Unraveling seeks to
Rebalance the inequities and
the inequities of the last generations.
Smug and cranky: short time horizons
Millennials, GenX'ers and early adaptors
Soon stride the Earth like velociraptors.
Humanity— Put your affairs in order.
Disorderly have affairs of ardor.
Bob Dylan's World War III Blues:
Last man on earth Propositions last woman, too
"Oh, No!" She says...
"Remember what happened last time!"

Scott Sherman

Ode to That Spark

Chemicals, ions, electric magnetic sparks
Descended from Quasars Pulsars and Quarks
You trigger my heart ignite my art
One magnificent network
to me immortal
since my start.

'Monkey-mind'? How dare you! I treasure each thought
Each moralistic dictum each Shouldn't and Ought
You guide me so deftly through this vale of tears
Though starting with nothing
I've lasted these years.

Oh explain, please, and clearly, just what is your goal
Each kitten each puppy each cub and each foal
To swagger and strut   emerge from that Ark
And reveal divine mystery that comes with this Spark?

Jo Ann Smith

Grave Matters

the two of us prescribed we
would be buried side by side
a seemingly prudent purchase
all those years ago
a pact made in youthful folly
thinking the future was ours to know

they summon me now
those two graves -
the empty one with my name on it
foreboding, even as it shadows
reveries of a love buried in the other

we never considered
one of us would die
as a puff blows out a match
in the amber sunrise
of our time together

we never imagined
loss would transform
to silver memory and
one of us would go on
to live another lifetime
move away and love again

what is the grip
of such an artless pact
by whose authority does it linger
compelling compliance

my bones cannot lie peacefully there
they would rattle for escape
yearn to become ash and drift
released in a northern wind
dust bound for dust
apostasy absolved

Jo Ann Smith

Emergency

never a place one wants to be
especially alone
my lifeline confined
to the parking lot

in a hurry they weigh me
no time to remove shoes
extra layers glasses ring watch
annoyed, my weight will be inflated

wheeled to a small single bed sterile space
medical charts are
thumb tacked in random order
to lime green walls
I eagerly respond to *you can lie down*

an air conditioner blows cold
my breath is labored and shallow
an invisible pressure on my chest
more terrifying than pain

blood pressure high
oxygen low chest tight
scar on my left breast placid,
but ever present

a masked nurse
I can only see her eyes
knocks, but does not wait for an answer
pushes a lab cart through the door

I tell her I'm a "tough stick"
and ask if she's the 'A Team'
she may have smiled, but she pokes a needle
and misses a vein three times -
once in my helpless, bloodless hand
before the A team arrives

blood finally flowing
I ask for a blanket
and am told I've put the gown on backward
it should open in the back, that's why you're cold
embarrassed I wonder if they flaunt this knowledge
as a trade-off for kindness
one leaves another arrives
pushing a different cart
complete with tv screen showing blue blips
and grainy green graphics

a re-run loop of my heart
the antenna stuck to pivotal parts of my chest
I think how convenient
to have the gown open at the front

more tests, some repeated
but mostly waiting
for another knock
that ignores an invitation

my mind keeps bargaining
that my life has been rich
and if this is the end
so be it

but I am terrified
not ready
too much to repair

happenings not to be missed
a heart not fully opened

tears roll into my mask
I can't pray
it seems so selfish to add one more plea
when God is clearly not coping

after six cold hours
colder still for my sweetheart
unplugged in the parking lot
I am discharged

poked prodded scanned
they think they know what it isn't
your doctor will call you
one more test
and we think we'll know what it is

Jo Ann Smith

The Only Girl

It was always hot on game day
and the soft dust around first base
blew like powder in the Santa Ana winds.
I was fourteen and knew everything
there was to know about softball.

After the fried chicken
corn on the cob
potato salad and chocolate cake
the women would clear and clean
while the rest of us headed to the field.

The guys would choose teams
and I was the only girl they'd let play.
Maybe I was the only girl
who wanted to play,
either way I had to be in the game.

I remember how the leather glove felt
when I slapped my fist into it
and ran out to my position at first base -
soft and pliable from the oil massage
I had given it the night before.

I knew softball — when to play in for a bunt
when to play back for a double play
how to put my heel on the inside corner
of the bag and stretch to catch the ball -
even when to call the infield fly rule.

I was fearless
moving with the grace of a toreador
as those grown men ran down the line at me
and the ball smacked my glove
before they flew past.

I can still feel the sweat
in my breasts and in my hair
and down my back and legs
preparing without knowing for the
big league games to come in my life.

Jo Ann Smith

I Never Saw It Coming

my eyes, wordless interpreters of intimacy
measuring the shape of light and dark
offering insight to my very soul
dart now like arrows here and there
their camera-like features snapping
pictures of what will become memory

but when I no longer see stars in a star-filled sky
when colors blend to blur
and magical fire offers nothing but burning and smoke
when all that was sharp loses its edge
and I can't see your eyes gaze into mine
or the contortion of my own tear-stained face
secluded in an immutable night
I can't help it, I think of my mom
whose grip on me was always too tight
and wish for just a moment of crying on her shoulder

Jo Ann Smith

Coming To My Senses

this-road ~~is~~ full of potholes
the streetlamp ahead is flickering
a power outage looms
the light is going out

no full moon will breach this dark
other senses lesser than sight
must wake-up in the mid of night
to face the witching hour

here in the Anza-Borrego desert
coyotes pace in crackling fallen palms
their unique yapping
alerts the curly canines I shelter

tense muscles tight as clenched teeth
a sense of force and velocity readies me
just in case   my body measures the space
between them and us

sunset has chilled daytime warmth
I enfold myself in a bearhug
feel the goosebumps
on my bare cool skin

smell the newly mown grass
where I used to play golf
imagine the smack of a 3-iron
on an elusive dimpled ball

mariachis margueritas infectious
happiness at the old Red Ocotillo
a dripping chicken quesadilla
swims in the juicy buds of my mouth

how many senses then do I need
how keen
if one is lost
can the others become

you hold my hand
a transcending sensation
an abiding guide
in a Cimmerian land

Linda Stamps

Dominant Chord

"A long blue unearthly note"
— Gail Entrekin

He scales the clef, trills and pops,
the key pads soft tap each note.
Cheeks bulging, he reaches the crescendo
and holds the pitch, an endless screech.

Sax player on Market Street
a short block from Zuni Café
homeless, smudged and soiled,
reeks of disregard.

A reclaimed jar holds change too spare, a few bills.
His chubby dog curls against the flat of a building,
its coat spotty against patches of mottled skin.

The aroma of spit-roasted chicken punctuates the scene.
A line long with the privilege of place pulses with anticipation
ruffling against the wail of his saxophone
bleating scales, warbling sharps and flats.
The whirr of traffic and blare of horns pierces
the tickle of grace notes.

I lean against a light pole, close my eyes and listen
to the plea and wail of riffs, and imagine a jazz club.
On a small stage he plays to a crowd
sipping drinks, drifting with the music.

I shudder and open my eyes,
wrap my coat tight against the chill.
I place a five in the jar
avoid his eyes as he nods.
His dog raises its head, ears erect,
too close, time to go.

Down the street, inside the café
I am greeted by a smile,
the warmth of an open kitchen
and a long blue note of dissonance.

Linda Stamps

Artifacts

A blood moon shadows the mesa —
ancient unmarked graves
host a cluster of dust spirals
the wind keens against the thud
of a silent drum.

A chorus of coyotes pierces the prickly pear,
each yip and howl rising skyward
slivers of light shimmer
the ghosts of elders reach
for pottery shards and mesquite,
a hint of smoke in the desert air.

The weavers struggle to knot the thread
of what was before the scatter and screams,
pueblo patterns dangling in shreds
of endless mending raveled and unraveled
by a loom of whitewashed bones.

Linda Stamps

Departure

I. Obitus (go toward)

packing the senses
only sound remains
coming and going
straddling currents
the in between
last words
hands held
vigil
breath rising   falling
pooling eddies
of lifeblood
heart's crescendo
forte to pianissimo
stillness
pronouncement

II. Mortuarius (pertaining to the dead)

announcement
mentor
purple heart
lifelong fan
collector
50th wedding anniversary
90th birthday
remembrance

III. Mortem Aestuarium (death's estuary)
rising
tide
meets
the
stream

Linda Stamps

Glyphs

the canyon cradles the river
snaking across the divide

a single red tail catches a draft
and rides the moment

sienna cliffs rise uneven toward
sun's blaze, the air brittle with heat

the hawk hovers and drops to an outcrop
talons tensed for the kill

the prey writhes, an ascent, a screech —
pierced silence

white water roils
toward the sea breaking open

Linda Stamps

Twelve for Dinner

> *"As our galaxy is getting older, it is getting fatter."*
> — Dr. Ting Li, physicist

The scientists say that the Milky Way's
feeding habits shine a light on dark
matter, and other matters, the super-
massive blackhole that gobbled up
a star in 1980 or the giant asteroid

3,500 feet wide hurtling toward earth
right now, while probes and solar
mirrors poke and prod planets, sample
Mars and reach for the edges of the
cosmic buffet.

Not guests, quests from gravity's pull
former galaxies shredded to a dozen
stellar ribbons feeding the Milky Way
as pulsars, the cosmos's blinking stars,
take measure.

Cosmovores of intergalactic cuisine
aging consumers expanding until—
perhaps, that's the source of the
Big Bang, the point at which
consciousness pulses.

Steve Trenam

At the Far End of a Sturdy Branch

for Fran Claggett-Holland

You, who knew Robert Frost,
and bought a Picasso
with money you didn't have,
now greet me at your door
with a Saluki and a Whippet,
in a dress windswept
with charcoal brush strokes,
a necklace which only
your neck could honor,
and a smile to welcome me in.

The house brims with art.
A collusion of couches and chairs
brace themselves to accommodate
an entire tribe of poets.
The butcher block, scored
with decades of Madge's slices
in concert with flour from your hands.

As you speak of your two only sons,
both poets grown grey,
and Madge behind a permeable
membrane of memory—
I hear the music of
"the end of your beginning,
measuring out the days
grounded in rhythm and rhyme."

At one point I envision you
holding a cup of hot chocolate,

marshmallows melting on the surface,
afloat on the second movement
of Beethoven's *Pathetique*.

While you leave a lifetime
of astonished poets in your wake,
(every encounter a potential student)
I catch a glimpse of what
my life could have been,
and might still become.

Steve Trenam

Silence

A skipping stone
at the bottom of a pond
waiting to sail

A photograph of a girl
plummeting minus her cries
and the flutter of her dress

The resonance of paintings
in crowded museums
after the brush strokes have dried

Goya's bright gunshots
aimed at Spanish loyalists
against a mound of dirt

A daughter bound to the mast
In Longfellow's Hesperus
waiting to sink

Mythical Washington
crossing the Delaware
shouting commands

The urban emptiness
beyond a wedge of glass
in Edward Hopper's *Nighthawks*

The crawling of beetles
over our quiet bodies

Steve Trenam

Lavender

Nobel Laureate poet
Joseph Brodsky
sometimes sat on a park bench
with Mikhail Baryshnikov
opposite a field of lavender.

He watched how it bent
clear to the ground
when it got full of itself.

He would snip, bundle, and hang
the lower branches from curtain rods
to gift its dried sunlight.

In summer, he would sit
waist-deep in lavender
to enjoy the smell
and the feel of its blossoms
fingering his face.
Inside his apartment, vases of it
stockpiled against the coming cold.

One morning, one of his veins
became prominent.
And days later,
a small stem protruded.

He could hide it under his clothing,
but soon there were
branches bearing buds.

When leaves began peeking
from his sleeves, and bees
followed him up the aisles,
his girlfriend took over his shopping.

He began eating less
and taking longer, cooler baths.
Before long, Brodsky was mostly blooms
and his feet resembled roots.

His girlfriend and Baryshnikov
planted him in the lavender field
in Washington Square Park

where every dark night
she would allow his branches
to caress her bare legs,
and she would sing Puccini arias—

*"Vissi d'arte, vissi d'amore.
Perchè me ne rimuneri così?"*

Dorm windows would open to her,
and on occasions, one might glimpse
the world's greatest dancer
walking a moonlit brick path,
carrying a watering can.

Steve Trenam

Stream of Consciousness

There is a freshwater stream
hidden in the ocean,
thought to hold trout larger
than the one that got away.

No one knows its edges
or what keeps the ocean at bay,
but its water is sweet and pure—
free of hooks and lures.

And although sailors
have caught glimpses
of it streaming
beneath their hulls,

I can only dream
about the sanctity
of trout in utero,
rolled up in ocean quilts,

as I walk along
this impoverished shore,
tasting salt.

Steve Trenam

Parabola

The dawn of her life
was unflawed
save for the tap
of a needle up her spine

It did not find
what it was looking for
and I placed her
in a Leboyer bath
to welcome her
with a poem

She had a salon's blonde
streak at her hairline
Her toes were splayed
and she kept extending
her legs as if reaching
for the stage

My mother
both hands on the glass
wore an unfamiliar grin
I would never see again

When she pivoted
into assisted living
her attention wandered off

As my daughter
was donning pointe shoes
my mother's mouth puckered

into a silent O
and her eyes became stones

She never lived to see
Stravinsky's fiery bird
Her granddaughter's legacy

One day I will spin
a final word
but I will have
seen her dance

I will have seen
her dance

Judith Vaughn

Shiva Birds

All night long we heard the shrill of one voice
dying. First, loud, pleading; silent for a brief
time; continued, waned.

My heart anguished at pain flung into the night,
a cry for help. I ventured into the dark, flashlight
in hand, a useless tool. Left on its own, the plead
faded to a whisper.

They came this morning when it stopped.
Black crows by the tens crying out a Shiva song.
Birds' prayer laid on the dead thing. A blanket
woven with years of instinct and ritual.

Grieving Shiva birds finished their adieu,
took flight to blue sky, waiting trees, living.
They never looked back.

Judith Vaughn

Day in the Country

Red sky morning; sun and moon face off.
Sonoma stretches and yawns. Golden
fields extend to the horizon, hawks
shadow above.

Ancient light travels from the sun, dances
on purple skinned figs clutching branches
laden with succulence.

Crows call out from tree tops in the distance.
Speaking in tongues, a foreign language
to my ears.

Steaming coffee on the counter, dog stationed
at the screen door. We all wait for something
before day moves into night.

Except the dog; he has one thing in mind: running
back and forth, squeaky ball in mouth, letting
the world know he is on guard.

Judith Vaughn

A Murder of Crows

walk in circles around a fallen friend
whose spirit flew into another world.
They pray for their departed like monks
in black robes.

In silence
they walk in collective memory of
her flight along side, her sound
distinct as a fingerprint.

In silence
they remember her call in early
morning as sun broke sky with light,
and their world diminished by one.

In silence
they remember her play, sliding down
a snow covered hill in the midst of
winter days darkening into a moon filled night.

Science suggests crows walk
in circles around their dead to learn
about predators and danger.

Some tribes celebrate their deceased
ancestors as crows. The Hopi celebrate
the Crow Mother as guardian of children and crops.

A murder of crows walk in circles around
a fallen friend, unaware, indifferent
to science, ritual or celebration.
They offer another kind of prayer to the departed,
I imbued with its own numinous divinity.

Judith Vaughn

I Have No Prayers

I was there for its last breath, the finch
who mistook the front window reflecting
trees as safe harbor.

I picked it up, held it gently, eyes blinked
once, twice, small breath, death. Another
bird waits in a tree for its return.

How is it this death can wrest my heart
in a million ways? The thud against the glass
a bird's requiem. I have no prayers or songs; just sorrow.

Judith Vaughn

Murmurations

Imagine driving toward coastal mountains
on a road next to a field of ripening grape vines,
with no expectations, looking at the afternoon
sun shining through after rain clouds so clean
no memory of other storms can mar its luminous light.

The view not familiar, though it rests in the heart,
reaching out hands to hold tightly the spirit of some
thing mysterious.   unknown.

On the horizon, starlings, a million black
cuts in light of sun and blue sky,
synchronizing, shape shifting into a swirling
liquid mass of artists with wings.

Imagine pulling over to the side of the road,
windows down, awe streaming into the day,
dancing into the sky with invisible flows of life energy.
The sound of whoosh, whoosh overhead, soft drumbeats.

Thousands of birds touching wings
as a single entity moving, twisting, twirling
on a canvas of light and blue.
Mysterious,   mesmerizing.

Marilyn Wolters

Amanda

Fat cheeks, her tongue held
Loose between her lips,
She breathes her mother's hum
And father's chat.

Their doting hands
Caress her satin flesh
That weeks ago
Left amniotic seas.

Tight-wrapped in fleece
She flings against constraint,
And punctuates the air
with tiny grunts.

She awaits the plump of breast
And the bull-eye surge of milk,
While wide obsidian eyes
Confront the blurry stubborn world.

Jaime Zukowski

In Memory Care

In the Memory Center where my mother dwells
a caregiver smiles and shares *Your mama has the body
of a Kenyan woman.* These past months since moving here
my mother's flesh has regained a youthful plumpness

but the sun-kissed freckles I remember of years past
no longer peek through. She cannot eat stand-up bathe
or attend to herself alone anymore. She can no longer
speak but stares into my eyes closely to say she hears.

This tender-hearted man tending to my mother tells me
of his last employment in Nairobi *Insurance Services*
he says. *I miss my mama too— so far away...* I watch him
lift his charge from her wheelchair to the soft flowered sofa

in the windowless but well-lit visiting space. My mother
eases into worn cushions. Her face that has forgotten
how to smile alights as she holds her gaze with the eyes
of her caregiver. With his grand smile to her I see new

roses bloom over lovely cheekbones—
my mother's *thank you*
in knowing once again
the comfort of a gentle man's arms.

Jaime Zukowski

Love's Lack

I couldn't see
inside the colorful shanties of Johannesburg
Missed the shadowed faces
under bridges in New Delhi
Sped by too fast to count
the soot-blackened dwellings
under smokestacks on the highway
Never witnessed the crumbling hillsides
of Rio de Janeiro— the opened arms
of Christ at sunrise

But in this rainbowed city by the bay
in early hours of dawn I saw
this waning year through my window
a stranger in front of the houses across the street
young male   body of my son   at the curb
a bent figure dwarfed by a toppled blue bin
sorting plastics
smelling licking tossing
remains

With my first cup of coffee
steaming between my palms
I watched tasted through my eyes
a disgust wet with shame
heat rising to silently observe
another human soul
move like the alley's raccoon
to finally find the last drops

Stood unseen
behind the glass pane
to see him carefully replace the empties
close the lid of the bin
shuffle in cement-torn slippers
to drag his bag
down the street
towards the new day's sun

Jaime Zukowski

Call

When you told me the whole story
that so many months had passed

since you couldn't get yourself to call
and let me know   I understood

In a way already knew something was lost
had heard the sigh in the message you left

Thought you'd had too much to drink   put off
my call   thought you might be here in town

felt it still too soon to get together
after all that's happened in a year

But I did call back and you let me know
that he was gone   that you both got sick

and he worse than you   dead
like so many others whom we did not know

And I knew how one might let nine months pass
to share one's greatest loss with an oldest friend

Could feel the pain in telling someone who knew
you years before you knew what loss could be

And after our long-awaited talk   the *goodbyes*
the *love-yous*   it was still morning

and exactly like the first awareness of pandemic
time began to slow back to its silent creep

I have not yet counted the months as I struggle
to begin written words to you in sympathy

Jaime Zukowski

The Male of the Species

after "Bling" fighting fish sculpture, Steve Trenam

This species
of the seas
demonstrate
their lustrous needs
to overpower
Showy males
will advertise
with endless feats
of domination

Then we have
the masculine
in the Poets
of the earth—
Not shy to show
for eyes and ears
strengths that swirl
so patiently
within

Jaime Zukowski

Elegy for Question Mark Oak

   at Mt. St. Helena

Long gone the lives nourished by your unending gifts—
all those who sat beneath your heavy arms to crush
your acorns with volcanic stone. Generations of birds
and deer, the massive bear that once roamed here.

Your summer leaves cooled stagecoach teams— waving
tails beneath your limbs. Miners stood around your trunk
with eyes to the hills— your closest kin for fuel they took.
Settlers, farmers cut and cleared— for orchards, vineyards

views, land deals. Dry season flames took brush and fir,
blackened your bark— still you endured. When windstorms
blew down from the mount your figure held its curve with
grace, while others cracked, pulled from the roots.

Through all these years of timeless sky— your opened crown
through which to see! Is it bow, or question you pose?
Are we to answer or to ask? As life will gather, then will pass
as moving shadows cross the mount.

Fran Claggett-Holland and Les Bernstein

A Journey Lighted by the Aurora Polaris

*"15 Chinese Elephants are on a long march north
and no one knows why."*

— *New York Times*, June 2021

forget the fallen
embrace the risen
the unexpected vision
exposes the hidden

beyond village and farmland
fifteen great lumbering endlings
move in heavy unrelenting folds
through the wrinkled gray

a fallen industrial world tatters ties
an unwarranted lacuna
stalls the engine of their ordinary
distance is now the imperative

singularity names them all
provides remembered diasporas
a heightened sense of new well being
a buffer of shared belonging

admit the hidden path to Polaris
guidance to be transmitted silently
by delicate vibrations whispered
into the elephant ear

with love,
Les and Fran

Appendices

Poet Biographies

Barbara Armstrong, a devotee of The Poetry Collective, is fascinated by the nuanced power of words and their intrinsic music. Her poems have appeared in numerous anthologies: (merit poet *Phoenix* in 2018, first place winner Redwood Writers poetry competition, 2021.) Diversions include storytelling, linguistics, Balkan music, construction and organic blueberry farming.

Judy Baker, the Book Marketing Mentor, helps busy business authors grow their audience and sell more books without going broke or crazy. Baker writes poetry, memoir, fiction, and nonfiction. She resides in Sonoma with husband Garry, four chickens, and loves to read in their bee-friendly garden.

Kitty (Catherine) Baker has long focused on fiction writing for young audiences. Originally from Minnesota, relocated to California in 2016, she has joined Marin County Poet Laureate Prartho Sereno's Poetic Pilgrimage for the past five years, exploring the power and playfulness of words, officially adding poetry to her writing repertoire.

Margaret Barkley is a poet, teacher, and curious observer of humans and nature. Her first chapbook *Ribs* was published by Finishing Line Press in 2021. She has an MA in Psychology with a focus on group facilitation, has taught at SSU and USF, and has led a writing group since 1999.

JoAnn Bell is a member of SRJC Adult Poetry Class. She has lived a life influenced by great artists, poets, sculptors and philosophers. She considers herself an ordinary person who has enjoyed extraordinary influences. Writing is her hobby which articulates her observations through the "looking glass."

Jory Bellsey has been writing poetry, prose, essays and op-eds for more than 5 decades. A keen observer of people provides the inspiration for his writing. Lately, he has been spending much of his time watching the news and yelling at his TV while listening to politicians continuously lie.

Les Bernstein's poems have appeared in journals, presses and anthologies in the U.S.A. and internationally. Her chapbooks *Borderland, Naked Little Creatures* and *Amid the Din* have been published by Finishing Line Press. Les is a winner of the 6th annual Nazim Hikmet Festival. She also was a Pushcart Prize Nominee for 2015. Les' full length book *Loose Magic* is available on Amazon.

Skye Blaine writes fiction, memoir and poetry, developing themes of aging, and coming of age, disability and awakening. She has pieces included in eight prose and four poetry anthologies and also has published a memoir and two novels. A third novel is forthcoming. She is a grateful member of The Poetry Collective.

Laura Blatt has worked as a website writer, a laboratory technician and a publishing company manager. Her writing has appeared in *The Poet, Theme, Lilith Magazine, California Quarterly*, and several poetry anthologies.

Abby Lynn Bogomolny is the editor of *New to North America: Writing by US Immigrants, Their Children and Grandchildren* and the author of the poetry collection *People Who Do Not Exist*. She teaches Creative Writing at Santa Rosa Junior College. Originally from Brooklyn, New York, she is grateful for Sonoma County's horizontal space.

Angel Booth lives in west Sonoma County. She writes memoir and DYI books, and with substantial arm twisting, poetry. A prose and poetry cancer memoir, and a memoir, *Sobering Thoughts,* are ready for publication, and her upcoming book, *The Art and Science of Healing,* will follow in the next year.

Catharine Bramkamp is a successful writing coach and author. She has published 20 fiction and non-fiction books, the most recent will be her poetry collection, *UnConscious Words* published by Dancing Girl Press in December 2022 She is a college lecturer and workshop facilitator. For more information: *www.Catharine-Bramkamp.com*

Robbi Sommers Bryant's award-winning books include a novella, seven novels, five short-story collections, and one book of poetry. Published in magazines including *Readers Digest, Redbook, Penthouse,* college textbooks, and many anthologies, Robbi's work was also optioned twice for television. She appeared on TV's Jane Whitney Show to discuss her article, "A Victim's Revenge." Besides writing, she is a professional editor. *robbibryant.com*

Marilyn Campbell writes fiction, poetry and, on occasion, heartfelt personal narratives. A native Californian, retired social worker, and a dual member of California Writers Club, she lives in Napa with her husband, Michael. Look for her and a description of her two historical novels, *Trains to Concordia* and *A Train to Nowhere,* on her website: CAMITZKE PRESS.

Simona Carini was born in Perugia, Italy. She writes poetry and nonfiction and has been published in various venues, in print and online. She lives in northern California with her husband, loves to spend time outdoors, and works as an academic researcher. Her website is *https://simonacarini.com*

Fran Claggett-Holland is a teacher, poet, dog-lover, who loves to see others' poetry dreams materialize. She has published four books of poetry (and many books about teaching literature and writing), but currently loves her time on Zoom with poetry and art events; she especially loves working with Les Bernstein in editing poetry anthologies for Redwood Writers. Her perhaps final book, *Under the Wings of the Crow, A Legacy of Poems, New and Selected,* will be out this year.

Penelope Anne Cole, is a children's author who writes poetry, short stories and memoir. Her work has appeared in San Mateo County Fair's Literary Stage, Tri-Valley Writers, SF Peninsula Writers, Redwood Writers, Napa Valley Writers, and High Desert Writers Anthologies. Ms. Cole tutors K-6th grade, crochets, gardens, and enjoys time with her daughter, two cats, and one dog.

Marlene Cullen offers inspiration to writers through her series of "The Write Spot" books. Marlene's blog includes writing prompts, places to submit writing, encouragement to write, and techniques to improve writing. Marlene is the producer of Writers Forum where diverse presenters chat about the craft and business of writing. *www.TheWriteSpot.us*

Joseph Cutler is a psychotherapist and beekeeper who lives in Sonoma. A member of Poetic License Sonoma, he has shared his poetry through Sebastopol Center for the Arts. He has been published in the *Sonoma Sun*. He is the co-author of *Scapegoats at Work*, with John Dyckman PhD. (Praeger 2003).

Patrice Deems, a native Californian began taking dozens of spiral notebooks out of the closet in 2017, when she joined the Santa Rosa Redwood Writers. Years of poetry, song lyrics, stories, family limericks and obituaries crowd the pages. There is even an "original" musical amongst them. No going back now!

Paul DeMarco has lived for 35 years on a 6-acre property near Petaluma. He began writing poetry when he retired three years ago from his career in non-profit finance. He is a member of Poetic License Sonoma, a writers group that reads monthly through the Sebastopol Center for the Arts.

Nancy Cavers Dougherty is the author of four chapbooks; the most recent, *Heaven is in Truckee*, published by The Orchard Street Press. Her love of the creative arts goes back to her childhood in Massachusetts. Nancy is an advocate for local programs in the arts and human services in Sonoma County.

Anita Erola, originally from Finland, is a bilingual dual citizen. Her writings have appeared in numerous anthologies, and her photography has won awards. She is looking forward to the end of the pandemic, attending open mics, and the freedom to travel again, especially to Finland when the blueberries are ripe.

Rebecca Evert is retired from a career in Health Information Management. As a performing member of Rumi's Caravan she supports the restoration of the oral traditon of poetry. In addition she serves on the boards of Providence St. Joseph Hospice and Justicewise, an organization dedicated to addressing complex social challenges. Rebecca is an urban farmer and an avid propagator of bee, bird and butterfly gardens.

Robin Gabbert has had poetry published in several Redwood Writer's anthologies and the California Writers Club Literary Review. Her book, *Diary of a Mad Poet,* received a 5-star review from Readers' Favorite which said her poetry, "profoundly captures her ardent desire for living and continues to address truths in the fewest words through figurative language, phrases, and rhythm."

Christina Gleason is a multimedia artist including fine art, music, film, photography and writing. She finds inspiration in nature with an appreciation of how the land informs through elements of grace and presence and where tangent and shape and perception form resonance and creation,

Joan Goodreau's books are *Where to Next?, Strangers Together: How My Son's Autism Changed My Life,* and *Another Secret Shared.* A Pushcart nominee, Joan has been awarded a Hedgebrook Writing Residency to complete her play, Covid Silence. Her poems, stories and articles have appeared in numerous reviews and anthologies.

Chlele Gummer, author, illustrator and poet, lives in Santa Rosa. She has been published in Redwood Writers Prose and Poetry Anthologies. She has ten children's books published on *Smashwords.com* which tell stories of Rufus, a Canada Gosling. She is currently writing a novel.

Karen Hayes lives in Sonoma County. She loves her cat, Healdsburg, Fort Bragg, rivers, and driving. Currently she has one book of poems published, River Stone. There are several boxes of half-done pieces patiently waiting for her to attend to them.

Pamela Heck is a writer, artist and special education teacher who writes memoir, short stories, poetry, and picture books. She had an Award of Merit in the 2020 poetry anthology, *And Yet*. Look for *Amazing Animals,* her illustrated non-fiction book for children due to be released later this year.

J.L. Henker is a writer, blogger and lover of all things fantastical, especially dragons. She is currently revising/editing a high fantasy novel, querying Sci-Fi short stories and collecting vintage cookbooks for a retro cookbook project. She was most recently published in *Open Your Mouth*, a speculative fiction anthology benefitting the National Women's Law Center (March 2022). Her career has included book seller, used/rare book buyer and bookstore manager. You can find out more at: *https://jlhenker.com* and follow her on Twitter @jlhenker.

Basha Hirschfeld has been a writer and a seeker all her life. She lives in west Sebastopol and teaches meditation at a retreat center which she developed to give people a peaceful place to get to know their own minds. She finds the process of writing poetry a path to self-discovery.

Dr. Jon Jackson is a retired psychiatrist and depth psychotherapist, and an award-winning poet. He is a former Chair of the Numina Center for Spirituality & the Arts. He currently facilitates a Rilke reading group sponsored by the Friends of the San Francisco Jung Institute. He also teaches courses on "Rilke's Letters to a Young Poet" and "A Psychological Approach to the Old Testament."

Mara Lynn Johnstone grew up in a house on a hill, of which the top floor was built first. She lives in California with her husband, son, and laptop-loving cats. She enjoys writing, drawing, and spending hours discussing made-up things.

Karl Kadie is a Santa Rosa poet and author of *Revenge of Nature, The Burning House,* and *Singing with the Storm.* His work has been published or accepted for publication in *Train River,* 2021 Redwood Writers Anthology, *The Santa Clara Review, The New Verse News,* and *Haiku Headlines.*

Anne Keck writes science fiction, fantasy, and poetry. She believes in ocean swimming, live music, public libraries, climate action, and Italian cooking as love. She and her husband raised three powerful daughters and the two of them happily live on Maui.

Briahn Kelly-Brennan is so happy to be elbow to elbow in this anthology with some of their favorite poets— several of whom are actually even friends of theirs and one is a close relative so really it's a family thing this anthology and who better to have in their family?

Crissi Langwell writes romance, women's fiction, and young adult novels that often feature strong female heroines. She volunteers as newsletter editor and social media maven for Redwood Writers, and serves on the board as secretary. She lives in Petaluma with her husband Shawn and their spoiled and sassy cat Cleo. Visit Crissi's website at *www.crissilangwell.com.*

Shawn Langwell graduated from San Francisco State University with a Bachelor of Science Degree in Marketing and Advertising. He is the immediate Past President of Toast of Petaluma, and President of Redwood Writers, a branch of the California Writers Club. Shawn is the author of the memoir *Beyond Recovery: A Journey of Grace, Love, and Forgiveness.* Several of his stories and poems have been published in anthologies.

Betty Les is a poet and zoologist, exploring everyday observations and experiences through a lens of mystery and connection. Her poems have appeared in Redwood Writers Anthologies, in *Reverberations: A Visual Connection,* in *The California Writer's Club Literary Review* and other works. Her chapbook *Just Enough to See* is in production by Finishing Line Press. Betty is a member of The Poetry Collective and had an Redwood Writers Award of Merit in 2018.

Sherrie Lovler is a painter and poet from Santa Rosa. She is an Art Trails artist and teaches Lyrical Abstract Painting online, locally and nationally. Sherrie's paintings and poems inspire each other, and are paired in her award-winning book *On Softer Ground: Paintings, Poems and Calligraphy. www.artandpoetry.com*

Roger C. Lubeck Ph.D. is president of the California Writers Club, a past president of Redwood Writers, and president of It Is What It Is Press. Roger's publications include 10 novels, 2 business books, business articles, stories, poems, prize-winning fiction, and two ten-minute plays. Visit *https://rogerclubeck.wordpress.com*; *http://www.rogerinblue.com*.

Steven Lubliner is the author of the political satire "Threeway" and the Hanukkah memoir "A Child's Christmas in Queens." He is a prize-winning poet and two-time Redwood Writers contest winner. His short plays have been performed by the Raven Theater, 6th Street Playhouse, and the Petaluma Radio Players. He lives in Petaluma.

Marianne Lyon has been a music teacher for 43 years. After teaching in Hong Kong she returned to the Napa Valley and has been published in various literary magazines and reviews. Nominated for the Pushcart Award 2016. She has spent time teaching in Nicaragua. She is a member of the California Writers Club, Solstice Writers in St. Helena California. She is an Adjunct Professor at Touro University Vallejo California. She was awarded the Napa Country Poet Laureate 2021 title.

Elaine Maikovska is a retired lawyer and active writer living in Petaluma, California. Her work has been published in *The Medical Liability Reporter, 95% Naked,* Redwood Writers *Vintage Voices,* the *Argus Courier,* and *Beyond Distance,* Redwood Writers Poetry Anthology. Two of her plays were produced for the Redwood Writer's Play Festival.

Catherine Montague is a writer and university lecturer who lives in Sebastopol. Recent publications include poetry in the Redwood Writer's *Crow—In the Light of Day, In the Dark of Night* anthology and the Center for Human and Nature's *Minding Nature Journal.*

Rod Morgan has an AAS degree in graphics with a minor in creative writing and journalism. His chosen genre are tales and poems, constructed to amuse, entertain and mystify. He jumbles fact and fiction together in unknown quantities, weird equivocations of memories, recollections, fabrications and tales of the absurdly askew.

Jennie Orvino is the author of *Poetry, Politics and Passion*: memoir, poems, personal essays, and a spoken word album, *Make Love Not War.* She works as a grant writer/consultant, blogger and freelance journalist whose articles have appeared in *North Bay biz* and *Diablo* as well as *North Bay Business Journal. www.jennieorvino.com*

Amy Pane spent much of her life in the wilds of northern Mendocino. Living close to the land, with the inherent isolation led her to words as haven. She uses them as a way to intimately connect with and communicate time, place, and emotion. She is currently writing poetry and memoir.

Linda Loveland Reid's writings and poetry have appeared in over 30 various publications, two novels available on Amazon. Linda teaches art history for SSU and Dominican University in their Osher Lifelong Learning programs. Other interests include figurative and abstract painting and directing community theater. Website: *LindaLovelandReid.com*

Jane Rinaldi's imagination had momentarily been dulled by COVID issues, ZOOM meetings, and masks. Recently, it has perked up a bit, and she hopes her returning interest in writing poetry will continue to re-expand and re-flower.

Margaret Rooney is a retired psychologist and former farmer with a positive addiction to poetry. Her two poetry groups help her manage this in healthy and metaphorical ways. Her poems have appeared in several Redwood Writers Anthologies, the *California Quarterly*, the *Ekphrasis Journal* and the *Blue Unicorn* and other journals. She won first prize in the Redwood Writers Poetry Anthology Contest and two of her poems were nominated for the 2020 Pushcart Prize.

Janice Rowley's curiosity has led her many places, from the rural South to the California wine country, from airline to veterinary, from show dogs to rescue dogs, from reading to writing, from memoir to poetry to fiction, from a young woman with dreams to an aged one with memories. Jan's prose and poetry have been published in various Redwood Writers annual anthologies.

Dmitri Rusov-Morningstar composed the poem "Meditation" in the early sixties as he left the security of childhood and entered adulthood at a terribly turbulent time. His despondency led him to a lifetime of political activism beginning with a career producing major folk music concerts and working the political movements of the day.

Kathleen Scavone, MA., is a retired educator. She freelances fiction, poetry, nature writing, curriculum ideas and local history. She has self-published four books, a play and a poetry chapbook. Kathleen is a photographer and potter. Her other interests include hiking, assisting on archaeology digs, travel and volunteering for NASA

Florentia Scott's poetry explores connections between perceived reality and imagination. Her work has appeared in various publications, including the 2018, 2019, 2020 and 2021 Redwood Writers' poetry anthologies, the 2020 prose anthology, and *Chicken Soup for the Soul: Listen to Your Dreams*. She was a 2019 Sonoma County Poet of Merit.

Scott William Sherman lives in Sonoma, where he has raised a family and run his Framery Wine County Gallery since 1973, publishing his graphic arts, framing and illustrating two geography books, and serving as Fine Arts Commissioner of Sonoma Valley. He initiated the Sonoma Art Treasures Award.

Jo Ann Smith spent most of her life in public education as a teacher, counselor, principal and superintendent — all at the high school level. In those capacities her writing relied primarily on the orderly left side of her brain. Now retired, she finds herself drawn to reading and writing poetry, a very different more satisfying kind of writing. This journey continues to be challenging, revealing and liberating. In 2019 Jo Ann was recognized as a "poet of merit" for poems published in Redwood Writers Poetry Anthology, *Crow*.

Linda Stamps etablished careers in law, journalism, and higher education. She also played professional football. Her published works include poetry, fiction, and non-fiction. She is a member of the Blue Moon Salon/Poetry Collective. Her poetry is inspired by a word here, a phrase there, and the endless horizon.

Steve Trenam teaches poetry writing for Santa Rosa Junior College. As a poet, he is neither sure-footed nor clear. Metaphorically speaking, Steve is out on a leafless limb with just spider webs and moss, listening to the silken slip of water over stone. Blue Light Press published his *An Affront to Gravity* last year, and his work has appeared in *Pandemic Puzzle Poems* and a collection of ekphrastic poems titled, *Canyon, River, Stone and Light*, both published in November, 2021.

Judith Vaughn lives in Sonoma, California. She attended New York City College, John F. Kennedy University, and Dominican University with a focus in Psychology. Publications: *First Literary Review-East,* an online literary publication; *Oak East New*s, a student publication at SRJC, in Santa Rosa, CA; and in *Jerry Jazz Musician,* publications.

Marilyn Wolters has lived in Sonoma County for over forty years. She spent most of her working years helping disabled college students develop essay-writing skills. Now retired, she can't resist writing regularly. Her poetry, short stories and short plays have been published and performed.

Jaime Zukowski earned a Master's of English, Creative Writing from the University of Colorado. Her column "At Home in Wine Country" was featured in the Weekly Calistogan before Zukowski's retirement from grape-growing. A former mayor, master gardener, actor and activist, Jaime shares poetry monthly with Sebastopol Center for the Arts.

Artist's Statement: Christine MacDonald

I was born and raised on the Isle of Tiree, a small remote island off the west coast of Scotland. It was the kind of place that lends itself to daydreaming and imagining, surrounded by the vast Atlantic Ocean, with limitless horizons and wide expansive skies.

Many of my paintings evolve from lingering childhood memories of that place and its unique atmosphere. Certain images appear consistently in my work — wild creatures and birds, often with a single human figure, boats and the sea — images which are both psychological and mythological, with layers of both personal and universal interpretations. They hint as well, towards notions of exile and homecoming, protection, tenderness, yearning and loss.

Now I live in the beautiful Valley of the Moon in Sonoma, and these months of lockdown and uncertainty, along with the recent wildfires, have made me even more aware of our relationship with the natural world. It might be that the lack of human companionship accentuates more than ever the value of of living here on the edge of the wild, and the sense of reverence for bird and beast, land and sea seems heightened, along with the gratitude and feelings of deep reverence that come when they cross my path or move into my field of vision. Glimpses from another world, animate or inanimate exchanges, separated by a chasm of otherness.

This is one aspect of the mystery of painting that brings me daily into my studio. Another is that the placing of colored pigments laid down on a flat surface can have the power to move us so deeply. Treading this pathway keeps me working, searching and yearning — it also fills me with hope, and wonder.

www.christinemacdonald.com

Redwood Branch History

Jack London was first attracted to the beauty of Sonoma County in 1909, the very year he was named an honorary founding member of the Berkeley-based California Writers Club [CWC].

In 1975 Redwood Writers was established as the fourth CWC branch, due to special impetus from Helene S Barnhart of the Berkeley Branch, who had relocated to the North Bay. She and forty-five charter members founded the Redwood Branch of the CWC.

Redwood Writers is a non-profit organization whose motto is: "writers helping writers." The organization's mission is to provide a friendly and inspirational environment in which members may meet, network, and learn about the writing industry.

Monthly meetings are open to the public and feature professional speakers who present a variety of topics on writing techniques, publishing and marketing.

The club sponsors a variety of activities, such as, Contests, Workshops and "reading" Salons. Over a dozen Writers Conferences have been held, offering seminars on various areas of writing.

Each year, Redwood Writers publishes two anthologies with prose and poetry, giving members an opportunity to publish their work.

In cooperation with the county's largest bookstore, Copperfields Books, Redwood Writers presents "Hot Summer Nights," where member's books are reviewed for discussion at meetings open to the general public. Also, Redwood Writers is present at the Sonoma County Fair, where members' books are sold and writing tips are offered to Fair attendees.

An extensive monthly newsletter and award winning website, along with other social media outlets, keeps members in touch with one another, to share accomplishments and successes.

Redwood Writers is indebted to its founders, to the leaders who have served at the helm, and to our many members. Without this volunteer dedication, Redwood Writers could not have developed into the professional club it is today with over 300 members. For more information, visit *www.redwoodwriters.org*.

Redwood Writers Presidents

Redwood Branch is indebted to its founders, members, and to the leaders who have served at the helm. Without their volunteer hours and dedication to the club's mission, Redwood Writers could not have developed into the professional and successful club it is today with over 300 members.

1975	Helen Schellenberg Barnhart	1992	Barb Truax (4 years)
1976	Dianne Kurlfinke	1997	Marvin Steinbock (2 years)
1977	Natlee Kenoyer	1999	Dorothy Molyneaux
1978	Inman Whipple	2000	Carol McConkie
1979	Herschel Cozine	2001	Gil Mansergh (2 years)
1980	Edward Dolan	2003	Carol McConkie
1981	Alla Crone Hayden	2004	Charles Brashear
1982	Mildred Fish	2005	Linda C. McCabe (2 years)
1983	Waldo Boyd	2007	Karen Batchelor (2 years)
1984	Margaret Scariano	2009	Linda Loveland Reid (3 years)
1985	Dave Arnold	2013	Robbi Sommers Bryant (1.5 years)
1986	Mary Priest (2 years)	2015	Sandy Baker (2 years)
1988	Marion McMurtry (2 years)	2017	Roger C. Lubeck (3 years)
1990	Mary Varley (2 years)	2020	Shawn Langwell

Awards

Jack London Award

Every other year, CWC branches may nominate a member to receive the Jack London Award for outstanding service to the branch, sponsored by CWC Central. The recipients are:

1975	Helen Schellenberg Barnhart	1998	Barbara Truax
1977	Dianne Kurlfinke	2003	Nadenia Newkirk
1979	Peggy Ray	2004	Gil Mansergh
1981	Pat Patterson	2005	Mary Rosenthal
1983	Inman Whipple	2007	Catherine Keegan
1985	Ruth Irma Walker	2009	Karen Batchelor
1987	Margaret Scariano	2011	Linda C. McCabe
1989	Mary Priest	2013	Linda Loveland Reid
1991	Waldo Boyd	2015	Jeane Slone
1993	Alla Crone Hayden	2017	Sandy Baker
1995	Mildred Fish	2019	Robbi Sommers Bryant
1997	Mary Varley	2021	Roger Lubeck

Helene S. Barnhart Award

In 2010 this award was instituted, inspired by Redwood Writers' first president, to honor outstanding service to the branch, given in alternating years to the Jack London Award.

2010	Kate (Catharine) Farrell	2016	Robin Moore
2012	Ana Manwaring	2018	Malena Eljumaily
2014	Juanita J. Martin	2020	Joelle Burnette

Additional copies
of this book
may be purchased at
amazon.com.

Made in the USA
Columbia, SC
09 June 2022